ALL YOU CAN EAT

In order to get a sense of what it is we currently eat, both at home and when eating out and about, I'll need to get a sense of what we buy, where we buy it, and what we cook when we've got it home. And in the same breath I'll need to find out what we want from our restaurants, which restaurants we want, which restaurants exist and who's going to which places.

My hypothesis before setting out is that we've become untethered from what British food might have been before the Second World War – local, regional, connected to the land and to farmers and fishermen, delivered to us via local shops selling local produce, or by cafés and stalls selling traditional British fare. If there was anything else, it would typically have leaned on the teachings and structure of Escoffier and courtly French dishes. For anything further afield you'd have needed to go to a city, and your choices would've been almost exclusively between Indian and Chinese food. Mostly, though, after a decade-and-a-bit of rationing, and before globalisation allowed us to ship produce fresh to supermarkets from all over the world, we were stuck with the sort of food your grandparents might have talked about, or that might have been served as school dinners before Jamie Oliver got involved. But, for the most part, you'd think that part of the culinary landscape was old money, cast away sometime in the 70s.

The second part of my hypothesis is that what has replaced that food culture has been a cornucopia of

Introduction

holidays, not a weeknight in front of the telly. If you want to understand what British food actually is, and where it's going, you need to take in the mundane and the ordinary. And so on my tours around the country I've focused on the villages I stopped in at random, the high streets and their chains, giving their standard fare – the new normal – as much credence as noted restaurants and worth-a-visit farm shops and delis. There is a huge amount to celebrate about British food, and I've come across villages, restaurants and shops that present the very best of it. But I've also spent time in hamlets served only by a One Stop or a Spar, or by butchers that cannot move local meat and rely on generic staples bought in from overseas for revenue; I've visited cynical restaurants and awful ones too, and great swathes of the country that have simply lost touch with what British food might once have been, but haven't replaced it with anything of note. Ready meals, quick fixes, processed meals are delivered as rote, unquestioning, uncaring, on all sides. I have rejoiced in how good things can be, how much we can care, how eclectically we can put together a bright vision of British food for the future, reflective of the land we farm and the people we celebrate as British. I have despaired though, too, watched us accept the very least effort, the very worst foodstuffs, the very laziest of approaches to feeding ourselves and our loved ones.

I won't ruin things by revealing all the gory details here, but I will let you in on what my hypothesis and methodology looked like before I set out on this journey.

a greedy cook and a writer. I've spent nearly twenty years travelling, eating and cooking food from all over the world in restaurants, developing dishes for recipe columns in national newspapers, and writing cookbooks that reflect our national habit of looking outwards and adopting cuisines from all over the globe. But until now, I have not ventured far enough within my own country to properly assess our own cuisine – and this is what I am here to address. When it comes to food, there's no feeling in the world greater than discovering a chef, a stallholder or even a corner shop that's doing something unexpected, unique and delicious. I've come across dozens of such people all around the world on my travels, and now I want to explore the truth about British food and uncover the food heroes shaping what our national cuisine looks like today – and what its future holds.

I have covered this country, top to toe, coast to coast, to find out what British food really is, now. This is not intended to be some sort of feat of endurance, and I've purposely avoided hitting the most in-demand spots, the places where you're guaranteed a knockout meal. Those are the exceptions. After all, dining in a Michelin-starred restaurant in the plushest village in the Lakes won't tell us much about the daily diet of a family in Coventry. There might be farms in the UK that rear prime Wagyu steak, or genuine wasabi that's miles sweeter and more pungent than the dyed horseradish we usually get with sushi, but these are meals for high

Introduction

Isn't British food meant to be bad?

From abroad, British cuisine has been much maligned. For decades, centuries even, we've been tainted by stereotypes that accuse us of being buttoned-up, class-obsessed, binge-drinking and Europhobic. Not all of that is unfair. But when people talk about our national cuisine – when it's talked about at all, that is – it's usually reduced to little more than a few regional highlights: fish and chips, chicken tikka masala, Yorkshire pudding, a quaint fondness for tea cakes and scones. But how many of us still eat like that, on a daily basis? British food might once have been all about stiff sandwiches and limp vegetables, but you only need to walk to the shops to see that the reality is quite different these days. We are the most diverse country in the world, with some of the greatest chefs and restaurants anywhere, and British food is far more exciting and inventive than stereotypes would have you believe.

For my part, I am a chef of at least some talent,

Contents

Introduction	1
1. Scotland	13
2. The North-East	47
3. Yorkshire	69
4. The North-West	101
5. Wales	125
6. The West Midlands	155
7. The South-West	177
8. The South-East	201
9. London	227
10. Conclusion	249
Acknowledgements	259

For Harriet and Cecil, my world

First published in Great Britain in 2026 by
Profile Books Ltd
29 Cloth Fair
London
ECIA 7JQ
www.profilebooks.com

Copyright © Ben Benton, 2026

1 3 5 7 9 10 8 6 4 2

Typeset in Sabon by MacGuru Ltd
Printed and bound in Great Britain by
CPI Group (UK) Ltd, Croydon CR0 4YY

The moral right of the author has been asserted.

All rights reserved. Without limiting the rights under copyright reserved above, no part of this publication may be reproduced, stored or introduced into a retrieval system, or transmitted, in any form or by any means (electronic, mechanical, photocopying, recording or otherwise), without the prior written permission of both the copyright owner and the publisher of this book.

A CIP catalogue record for this book is available from the British Library.

Our product safety representative in the EU is BGC Sustainability & Compliance, 7 avenue du Général Leclerc, Paris, 75014, France. https://baldwinglobalconsulting.com

ISBN 978 1 80522 152 4
eISBN 978 1 80522 154 8

THE SEARCH FOR A NEW BRITISH MENU

BEN BENTON

Profile Books

Introduction

foods brought to us by people moving here from elsewhere, brought home by us from travel overseas or brought to our attention by the marvel that is the internet. I see this in the city where I live and work. But does it play out in reality?

Before I set off, I came across a rather wonderful film broadcast by the BBC in 1969 about 'exotic foods'. A quote from the feature really stood out: 'nowadays the humble potato sits side by side with sweet potato, yams, plantains, red and green peppers, aubergine …' Nearly sixty years later, it sounds ridiculous to consider the list above as at all exotic. Peppers and aubergines exotic? Surely not. They're not native to us, though, are they? They came from elsewhere at some point, and yet they're among the most commonplace veg we have today. So what else has trodden this path from gasp-inducing exotica to ubiquitous family shop fodder?

Another BBC segment is equally revealing – this time, it's about something much closer to home: crisps. Taking something so simple, it's a good example of how ready or resistant to change we can be.

The report, from 1981, starts with this introduction: 'Crisps were once plain, and then salted, and now they have the most extraordinary flavours. So Paul went out on the streets with gammon-flavoured crisps and prawn cocktail-flavoured crisps and pickled onion-flavoured crisps, the lot, and asked people if they could tell what the flavours were supposed to be.'

We cut to a typical British high street, a gaggle of old

ladies gathered round to try what the man has for them on his big orange tray. The first lady takes a crisp and chews. Her face is a picture of pursed lips and disgust, although there's a little latent intrigue, too.

'Tastes a bit fishy,' is all she can muster, before the presenter tells her the flavour. 'They weren't bacon,' she says. 'No way.'

The next flavour is chicken.

'Chicken? Never,' she says. 'They don't taste right. Not like the chicken I do. It's not coq au vin, is it?'

In that moment, I am hooked. This is forty-odd years ago, granted, but forty-odd years on from the Second World War, and hundreds of years on from the first immigration to the UK from China and the Indian Raj, thirty years on from the meaningful waves of post-war immigration to this country from China, India and the Caribbean, and flavoured crisps are strange and suspicious. Of course, we know all too well that flavours as advertised in crisps are synthetic tastes of real foods, much as we love the flavours we love. That this wonderfully expressive woman cannot fathom a chicken-flavoured crisp, but then uses a rather middle-class French chicken dish as her reference point to understand them, gives us an idea of how narrow – or perhaps how broad – our tastes once were.

This clip only becomes more surreal. Once this chipper woman is finished, we get a typical bloke, with a knitted baby-blue polyester flat cap, the type of mouth that can be folded up and over itself so that it

Introduction

can produce a gurn that might grace the front of postcards in bleak-grey seaside towns.

When asked to sample a crisp and decipher its flavour, this savvy cove says, 'You tell me what it is, I'll confirm it.'

The interviewer doesn't give in that easily. The chap tries a crisp and is given a prompt: 'It has two legs.'

The old boy takes a guess. 'Frog, is it?' Which, given a frog's clear and countable four legs, is an interesting choice.

The interviewer ploughs on. 'It flaps its wings.'

'It does?' queries the old boy, masticating again to gauge the likely flavour, 'Butterfly?' he says, straight-faced.

'Chicken.' The interviewer puts him out of his misery, but the mundanity of the flavour doesn't lessen the shock on the chap's face. 'Try another?'

'No, I don't want to,' the old boy demurs, before popping the next crisp in his mouth.

'This one hasn't got any legs at all,' the interviewer prompts.

'Not snake, is it?' And we're done.

It's a funny clip, but crisps are a universal British food – something almost everyone eats regularly, and as I sat with my bags packed, ready to begin my journey, I found myself thinking about what crisps tell us about how our tastes have changed over the years. To this old gent, the idea of new-fangled flavours conjures up the unimaginable – frog, butterfly and snake – so improbable would chicken, prawn cocktail and pickled onion be; but any other cuisine but our own was just as improbable. We might be a forward-looking nation, with the world's fare on our doorstep, but how recent is that phenomenon? How far are ordinary people willing to push their boundaries and adopt new things into their daily diets?

In the 1980s, we moved from a nation of plain crisps to one where the top five best-selling flavours were Ready Salted, Salt & Vinegar, Cheese & Onion, Prawn Cocktail and Beef, in that order. Meaty flavours were on the rise – and Monster Munch were the hottest innovation in town.

By the end of the 1990s, we'd seen the complete demise of the Ready Salted crisp; in its place Cheese & Onion reigned supreme, with Salt & Vinegar (or Salt & Lineker as it was known for a short period in 1995), BBQ Beef, Worcester Sauce and Pickled Onion rounding out the top five. This was the period of Walkers' 'Do Us a Flavour' advertising campaign, to encourage the nation to take risks on the exciting and the new. Which they clearly were, but still, nothing from any foreign cuisine was troubling the top of the leaderboard.

Even more shocking is that by the end of the 2000s, Cheese & Onion held firm as the most popular British flavour, with Salt & Vinegar, Prawn Cocktail and Roast Chicken below it. We did in the 2000s have a historically exciting development in British crisp history: the emergence of Thai Sweet Chilli-flavoured crisps, largely

Introduction

through the perennially present 'Sensations' line from Walkers, as the third most popular crisp of the decade.

That by the end of the 2010s the only change in the top five is that Smoky Bacon has replaced Roast Chicken as the fifth most popular crisp in the country is a sad indictment of our flavour incuriosity. And that in the 2020s the top three are unchanged – though Roast Chicken has ousted Prawn Cocktail and Smoky Bacon, and a medley of crisps labelled as some spicy derivative of 'Flamin' Hot' has taken fifth place on the list – is more damning than I might have hoped. We are lazy traditionalists, that's my new hypothesis. We took the 70s' and 80s' evolution in time-saving culinary developments into our hearts, gave up on any culinary tradition that needed patience or a cultured palate, and instead found a comfy corner of our culinary history that let in Anglified Asian food and not much else. At least where crisps are concerned, we haven't changed much since then.

Am I being hyperbolic? Perhaps. And how does our taste in crisps dictate this to me? Well, nothing is lower risk than the purchase of a bag of crisps. Standing at your butcher's counter and faced with something unknown, or looking up at a wall of spices in the supermarket that promise dark, deceptive or threatening ways to flavour your supper, I understand that caution might be applied as hard-earned money is prised from your frigid paw. But a bag of crisps? Surely you'd be willing to risk it all for a fun new flavour.

Returning to my research, perhaps the problem lies not in what we want but with what we're offered. What was the most radical experiment in crisps? In the 1980s, hedgehog-flavoured crisps were a genuine flavour brought to market, based on a false claim that Romani people ate hedgehog. So far, so mad and racist. And perhaps this single crazy development put us back half a century at least: the 1990s saw Ketchup, Branston Pickle and Worcester Sauce as the three most radical innovations, before Full English Breakfast and Chocolate (and Chocolate & Chilli) were tried in the 2000s, and Haggis & Black Pepper, Brussel Sprout and Cajun Squirrel in the 2010s. That's right, Cajun Squirrel, proving that despite hundreds of exciting, diverse and delicious cuisines being represented in Britain, Walkers still decided that an outdated gimmicky view of Cajun food might unlock a new fervour among British crisp eaters.

It's only in the last five or six years that Katsu Curry, Coronation Chicken and Black Truffle have been trialled on the British public, which, though not radical by any stretch, are at least attempts to reflect flavours and dishes that are popular in the UK today.

Hopefully the rest of our diet has been a bit more interesting. We have certainly moved beyond what our grandparents ate, but how far we've come is unclear. As new people and new cuisines have arrived in the UK, we have adopted some dishes, bastardised others, or – in a few exceptional cases – found a way to bring new life

Introduction

to tired classics. Many factors come into play, not least immigration and globalisation; but foreign holidays are more ubiquitous now, and taste is driven as much by the internet and what property developers and investors think is on trend as by tradition and availability.

I will start as far north as I can, in Cromarty, a few clicks north of Inverness, and zigzag down the country from there. I suspect I will sometimes find what I'm looking for, but will often be left disappointed and having to redraw my conclusions. I already know that I am bound to be struck by certain tensions. The good intentions behind fighting to save traditions from extinction versus the knowledge that many of these aren't worth saving. Alongside this there is the tension between those traditions and the innovations that threaten them, and the idea that innovation for innovation's sake is a good thing. I can tell you now: it's not, at least not always. We have limitless choice in our supermarkets, but the vast majority of us have our buying habits dictated to us by supermarket supply chains and the whims of marketing and buying teams, themselves responding to gusty trends on the internet and in wellness movements. I have a sneaking suspicion that we're keen to try more than we're often offered, that young Brits are open to the new, but that supply doesn't satisfy demand outside of the big cities, and that a loss of cooking skills means we're not sure how to experiment. I won't be delving into education policy, nor governmental failures on school food and the national diet, but I will be presented with these issues in many places.

As someone who produces and consumes food media for a living, I know the grand stories we tell; all of them are true in essence, but most are sadly limited in reality. I just hope the balance tips in the favour of progress, of more of these positive developments being true than not. I will not shy away from reality, though. I promise to say it as I see it.

And so, as I load the last of my luggage into the boot of the car and start the journey north to Scotland to begin the slippery slide through Britain's culinary landscape, what snacks do I have for the drive? A prawn cocktail sandwich, a big bag of Takis Fiery Hot, a big bag of Crinkle Cut Salt & Vinegar crisps, a pack of mini pork pies and a two-pack of Scotch eggs. Wish me luck.

1

Scotland

The problem with Scotland is that it is all too good up there.

An extraordinary country for food and drink, it's too far north for wine, but that aside, it is better for the raw ingredients we need for our tea than anywhere else in the country. You want the best seafood in the British Isles, who are you calling? A hand-diving-for-scallops Scot, or a langoustine legend, or a gang out in the North Sea hauling up mackerel, herring, haddock and cod. And that's just on the East coast. If you're heading out west, the fishers in the Hebrides will tell you all you need to know about crab, lobster, oysters and mussels, not to mention pollock, whiting and the mighty monkfish, its face like a seafaring scally too intimate with the bottle. Away from the sea, the cattle, game, venison and lamb are as tasty up there as you'll find anywhere. Between late winter and early spring, leeks, potatoes, turnips and brassicas soften the hunger gap, though there's always whisky to keep you warm – and there's always the supermarket. You'll eat as well in

Scotland as you can hope to eat anywhere in the world. And I haven't even mentioned the raspberries.

And yet, from where I sit now, the Scottish still have to fight tooth and nail to distance themselves from the deep-fried pizza supper, the only country in the world where another soft drink, Irn Bru, outsells Coca Cola, and the perennial tarring that was the deep-fried Mars Bar. How easily we pigeon-hole.

Whether Scotland will set the tone for what British food is all over the country, I am yet to find out. I want to know what Scottish food is today, and perhaps how much good Scottish produce gets immediately exported to London, and abroad, and how much is still available to the locals. What I can tell you is that for every extraordinary small producer making something very good in Scotland, be it beer, whisky, marmalade or local cheese sold through a thriving network of farm shops and butchers, there is a Scotmid, Londis, Costcutter or Spar that would make you weep if you had to survive off it day in, day out. Scotland being as rural as it is in parts, you encounter far too many of these 'convenience' stores in low, grey towns and villages. That's not a phenomenon unique to Scotland either. Later on my journey I'll have run-ins with similar stores in Wales and the Lake District, but it often seems that the more scenic and bucolic the place you're in, the more dire the immediate food offering.

Before all of that, though, let me welcome you to Cromarty. North of Inverness, this little seaport sits at the tip of the Black Isle and the mouth of the Cromarty Firth. Its industry was in North Sea oil platforms and more recently building wind turbines. Alongside that grit and graft it's a tourist town, and a nice spot for it too. It has all the hallmarks. A nice little cinema, a third wave coffee shop, a pizza place, a deli, a very good ice cream parlour or two and a few tea rooms. It is a lovely day out, especially if you're into decommissioned oil rig platforms, as these wash into view every now and again while they're being towed into port from out there. 'There' being the North Sea, for that is what Cromarty backs on to, if you crane your neck as you stand at Slaughterhouse Coffee waiting for a very good black filter coffee with which to start your day. The problem with Cromarty, specifically as someone keen to understand what British food is from the perspective of those living here, is that it has its shit together, which means its outward face is almost too perfectly packaged for me to take it at face value. There is a popular spot called Sutor Creek, positioned at a crossroads within sight of the Cromarty ferry. Most visitors here will have to walk past it, and many will be drawn in by the menu, which reads like a who's who of Scotchanalia: Cullen skink with oatcakes, Haggis bon bons with a whisky mayonnaise, crab pâté with Highland crackers. The main courses seem to be a celebration of local seafood, and there is the Sutor burger, which sees a caramelised patty stacked with lettuce and bacon before being shrouded in melted Smoked Dunlop, a local nutty cheese smoked over oak. They may as well make it wear a sporran and a ginger wig for all it's been perfectly rendered as a wee Scottish restaurant by the sea. That there is also a genuinely credible wood-fired pizza offering at Sutor Creek – and that only one of the pizzas has haggis on it – tells us this lot know what they're doing, giving the people what they think they want while avoiding obvious gimmicks. Is this an indication that up here, north of Inverness, the local diet is local, seasonal, classics with a modern twist? Certainly, the Scotmid we rummaged around in Avoch before driving out this way would suggest anything but. So we stop, as everyone does, and we order some pizzas to eat on the sea wall, and we listen (as one must when building the courage to question strangers about their eating habits) – and sure enough the accents are English, American, Canadian and German. This is not to undermine that things are nice up here, or that at the first stop on this journey down the British Isles, good Scottish produce doesn't showcase the best of place, to locals or visitors alike. It's surely possible to cater to both, but I want to know what the general British diet says about what we eat. I want to know what a local menu looks like when it is designed to attract those who live and work here.

I'm stopping while up here with a friend who I met when we worked together in kitchens in London in the early 2010s. He is one of the finest pastry chefs of his generation, a cynic and very fine cyclist – and as befits a man with that pedigree, he has turned his back on the food world and moved up here to live mortgage-free and unencumbered by the nagging wants of urban life. He has a speedboat, for god's sake, and we'll go out to play with dolphins in the bay outside his house before this stop is out.

For now, though, we're driving out of Cromarty and heading towards a few places selling food that Neil assures me is very good, made and used enthusiastically by those who live up here as part of 'normal' life, and reflective of British food too, in these parts at least.

First stop, a farm shop. Bucolic, farmsy, and empty. Except for us, of course. Two chefs, veg fanciers, marvelling at the Romanesco cauliflower, the little turnips, boring to most, crying out for a glossy cider glaze to us, the squashes to be roasted, skin on, garlic, fennel seeds, chilli flakes, oil and salt the only things needed, the regal plumes of cavolo nero, the humble largesse of a perfect hispi cabbage. In an adjoining room there are honeys and jams and condiments and biscuits and flowers and chiller cabinets of drinks and cheeses and charcuterie; over there, where you pay, is meat, and beyond, a freezer where there is more meat and some cottage-garden ready-meals that a crofter's wife seems to have cooked and packaged.

It will come as no surprise that we leave with a cardboard box piled high with plunder, veg mainly, and get back on the road. We drive a short while on a meandering road through flat farmland broken up by occasional thickets of woodland on the horizon. The sky is big up here, and we pass a tractor laden with massive swedes, and then soon after another trailer, parked in a field, the back door open and the trailer inclined so that the swedes tumble out for the waiting sheep to feast on. It makes me glad we didn't invest in swedes at the farm shop, and it also makes me reflect on the pragmatism of farmers, and the struggle too.

Before long we pull into a village, typical of these parts with low, hefty-bricked houses, overwhelmingly grey, even though most of the town is painted red and cream. We park up in front of a pub rendered white with black-painted windows and woodwork, as is the house style up here. Over the corner entrance there's a sign secured to the front of the place that depicts the name of the pub, the Anderson, emblazoned in bright red, across the face of a man who looks like he's just seen someone raised from the dead. I look at Neil, he stares back at me, smug, and rolls down the car window. I was expecting the crisp scent of salty air, but instead the streets of Fortrose are rich with sweet woodsmoke and the lip-twitching whiff of rendered animal fat hitting embers.

There is not a soul on the street in Fortrose, the village we're in, but entering the Anderson through the car park, a grand fiesta is being played out in this gravel courtyard with its few cursory picnic tables. It's as if the whole of East London is up here on a jolly. The beards are less intentional, sure, and the sartorial stylings more Iron-Maiden t-shirt and worn lumberjack shirt than the primped and rolled workers' jeans and Birkenstocks of East London, but the energy, the proudly gripped esoteric beer, the are-you-sure-you're-in-the-right-place-big-boy looks from the locals are all prime Hackney.

Before long, the story of the place emerges, but before that I am discombobulated by the signs that proclaim 'beer garden, whisky bar, pub, smokehouse, restaurant and hotel' and a menu that offers chicken wings, BBQ platters, burgers, superdawgs and Philly cheesesteaks.

Inside, the madness continues. There are over 250 whiskies behind the bar for a start, as well as beers from Belgium, Ireland, Germany and Holland. Neil handles our order, which I soon learn should always be the same thing, if you know what is good for you. Go to the Anderson and simply order each and every chicken wing on offer, which on that day meant robust well-bred wings fried and doused to perfection in Classic Buffalo sauce, BBQ Boss sauce and Guava Boss sauce. They will arrive in a red plastic basket, as they might in the US, and each will have a complimentary scattering of chillies, spring onions, sesame seeds and the like.

For our part, we retire to the car park and chance upon a recently vacated table so as to bask in what a joyful spot this is. I won't bore you with our reminiscences of good times in old kitchens, but soon enough the wings arrive. As they materialise it is as if the clouds part, an early evening sunshine bathes us in a soft sepia glow, the breeze settles, and with it the chatter softens. The scent of smoked meat hangs above us, another round of beers is magicked on to the table, the first bite of a Guava Boss wing is taken and all is still for a moment.

'So this is what you're all doing up here? Guava Boss sauce!' I shout at Neil through a mouthful of this extravagantly sauced wing.

'The lad's American – no surprises there. Obsessed with whisky. Loves his BBQ. It's good, isn't it?'

And it is good. I'm on wing three and the saucing is all on point; the sourcing of the wings is no doubt spot on too, if their muscular heft is anything to go by. I forget to ask about the provenance of the birds, so message Neil later and put the query his way. 'Probably, yeah, knowing them,' is his answer. And that's good enough for me.

'You've done me like a kipper,' I say, back in the moment and reaching for yet another wing. 'This couldn't be further from haggis bon bons and new ways with neeps.'

Neil smirks and lets me complete my own thought.

I have the whole of the country ahead of me – below me even, as my twisted logic sees it – and already I'm seeing a flaw in my theory about British food. Talk to anyone who's interested in finding authentic cuisine, and you'll find them separating into two camps. One holds that we should preserve what we once had, go deeper into the traditions of our cuisine and make sure nothing is lost. At that pole one might hope to zigzag down the country finding producers, earnest restaurateurs and home cooks, hobbyists and obsessives who are fighting progress and mass commodification, so that a version of British food as it once was still exists. At the opposite pole, the one I naturally lean towards, there is an excitement about reinvention – about what British food has become in the midst of immigration and the eye-opening impact of globalisation that has transformed what we eat, what we crave to eat and what we can buy as demographics have shifted. At this pole a food obsessive hopes to find new cultures such as Syrian, Sudanese, Somalian and Malaysian represented alongside the Chinese, Thai, Vietnamese, Indian, Sri Lankan and Bangladeshi that have influenced British food in the last couple of decades. This pole wants to find tikka masala ousted by roti canai, or chow mein by injera, in our national ranking of the most-eaten dishes. The truth is, of course, that tradition and innovation can and do coexist all over the country. Both poles are visible at the same time in certain places – and this is thrilling. What happens, though, is that this yearning for a hypothesis to be true leads to an overly specific itinerary, so that in the end you seek out the few spots that fit the view you want to see and overlook the reality of a place. You end up a tourist in a nice hotel in an 'exotic' location who wants to experience the 'real' lives of a place and so takes a guided tour to 'traditional' villages, when in reality you'd get a more authentic experience if you simply took a bus or two, stopped in the roadside cafés and bought from the regular shops and stalls that locals use. It might not deliver such an aesthetically curated view of a place and its culture, but the mundane will inevitably gift you a couple of pleasing surprises and a fistful of run-of-the-mill interactions from which you can glimpse what a place is like, what the people buy and eat and how they go about their business.

And so, with three baskets of wings eaten, the red baskets licked clean, I am reminded again that there is going to be much on this journey that challenges what I hope to find, and it is often going to be miles better than what I could have expected. I thank Neil for his services to Scottish food, for encouraging me to stop expecting Scotland to be a neatly packaged tourist flyer and instead a place like any other, a place where people crave chicken wings more than haggis bon bons, and shop in Scotmid as much as in the delis with thistles or tousled-haired cows as part of the branding, and for doing so by showing me as much, as opposed to simply rolling his eyes or berating me every time I made a faux pas or an excited observation that suggested as much. Tradition, experimentation, mid-range supermarkets – it's all here. And an American in an otherwise sleepy Scottish town has blown my socks off with the best chicken wings I've ever eaten. Is this evidence of both poles being present at the same time? Perhaps. Feeling optimistic, I head home for a nightcap before more of the same tomorrow.

Scotland

*

The following morning we're back in the car, heading towards Inverness. And then to a place called Findhorn, where we park behind sand dunes before walking up to a horsebox with a view of the North Sea.

'What treats do we find here?' I ask, slightly confused as to what could possibly be served out of this matte black apparition, but after last night's lesson with the Anderson I'm hoping to be pleasantly surprised.

'We won't be eating here,' Neil says, another smirk on his face as he opens the door to reveal a sauna, replete with huge picture windows taking in the rippling gunmetal grey of the North Sea beyond us.

Greedy and in the mindset of a food writer on the hunt, I have no words, simply flashes of panic with regard to boxer shorts, towels and the impending cold of the inevitable post-sauna dip in the sea.

'There's a pub that does very good mussels,' Neil says, giggling as he notices my panic. 'The sauna will have us ready for a feed.'

The mussels are indeed good, as is that night's supper from our farm shop bounty, and the good bread and homemade blackcurrant jam we breakfast on the following morning. Our first stop that day was a bakery in Rosemarkie for an exemplary croissant, not exactly a necessity after the bread and jam, but a pure joy all the same. And, more importantly, the first pin in my new culinary map of Britain, now pockmarked by similar spots selling glossy pastries and organic coffee.

The explosion in artisanal bakeries has been one of the most consistent developments I've noticed up and down the country, a change for the good I'd say, or – if a more disapproving sobriquet feels appropriate – a change for the trendy. In all but the remotest corners of the country you'll find somewhere to grab a nice coffee and some sort of croissant or pastry, which certainly wasn't true a decade ago.

One must push on, delightful though it would be to continue bakery hopping. And I have to make it to Edinburgh – via whisky country – in time for the rest of my appointments this side of the border, before heading further south. And so with the Black Isle in the rearview mirror, I drive south, one last instruction from Neil in my ear: 'Make sure you stop at the Horn.' Of course the obtuse bugger gave me nothing more, just as I pulled away, so I couldn't do anything with his information until I next stopped, which as bad luck would have it was nowhere near the Horn, which turned out to be a Fifties diner on the way to Perth with a massive cow on its roof, renowned for serving the best bacon sandwich in Scotland. Instead, I found myself in Dufftown, the home of Glenfiddich, among other notable whiskies and distilleries, and a place that surely couldn't be more Scottish if it tried.

The truth is, Dufftown is a place where one needs a designated driver, or a taxi, or at the very least a whisky jacket to brighten one's walk. The fumes alone when you take a distillery tour could tip you over the legal limit, and when you have an inclination to taste every whisky proffered your way in the name of informative tour guiding, the road is best avoided.

So it is that I carry on through Dufftown towards the Fife Arms, a pub with restaurant and rooms owned by Hauser & Wirth, the Swiss gallerists-cum-restaurateurs, who I've read have recently opened this place in Braemar, which I reason might be a good spot to stop for some lunch.

'Surely you'd rather seek out a local spot owned by locals offering local food in order to get a sense of what British food is to the locals in this locale?' I hear you hissing. And yet here I am, bowling into the Flying Stag, the bar of the Fife Arms, pleased to be presented with a menu and a pint of fresh lime and soda. The thing is, this is Distillery Town, and much like the Lake District, Disneyland or a medieval re-enactment at Hever Castle, often traders pitching themselves as traditional and local are nothing of the sort. Instead, the core of their business is aimed at hungry day-trippers who are desperate for traditional Scottish fare to accompany their building whisky headache, and who are more likely to go for something that sounds authentic and convincing when loudly recounted to friends on their return to America, Japan or Frankfurt.

My reasoning for stopping at the Fife Arms was that it would make a better choice than any number of tourist traps. My logic follows that if you're famous

Swiss gallerists opening a spot in whisky country, you'll likely employ a very good local kitchen team who'll be able to provide plenty of the aforementioned Scottish tradition delivered with good local Scottish ingredients. And having compiled that team, they'll likely want to show their worth by referencing the newer trends in dining that will make the place popular with affluent travellers passing through and locals out on the town. All of which, I am delighted to report, plays out beautifully as I scan the menu and read such delights as 'Porridge sourdough bread & cultured butter', 'Smoked mackerel pâté, burnt apple and oatcakes' and 'Argyll smoked trout with celeriac rémoulade and potato rösti'. That the menu lurches in a controlled fashion between Tain Minger, a wonderfully stinky cheese from north of where I've just been, and 'Comeback sauce', a piquant fried-food-dunking-sauce that is mainly ketchup and mayonnaise and hails from Mississippi (another American import), it becomes clear that good Scottish ingredients are good and Scottish and very much part of how people eat day in, day out – but also that chorizo, curry sauce and chimichurri are things that have been adopted into the culinary lexicon. I have some smoked mackerel pâté (exceptional, not overly smoky but piquant from horseradish, no doubt local and freshly grated) and a yielding beef cheek pie (heavenly, tasting deeply of aged beef and with every muscular sinew rendered to unctuous softness), before getting back into the car and heading deeper into the

Highlands to meet some friends with whom I will stay in the Cabrach before continuing my journey south.

The Cabrach is a largely depopulated rural community in Moray, or, to place it in more recognisable geography, to the south of typical whisky country and north of the Cairngorms. The Cabrach was once home to a huge amount of illicit whisky production and smuggling, and its long history of illicit whisky stills made it hugely important in the development of the legitimate malt whisky industry in these parts. Otherwise, the primary pursuits were agriculture, peat-cutting and hunting.

On the edge of the Cabrach is a roadside tavern named the Grouse Inn. As far as I can tell, they don't serve any food – but it's worth a stop because it has one of the pre-eminent collections of single malt whiskies anywhere in Scotland. It's run by the widow of the man who built this collection, a woman who doesn't drink, doesn't see what all the fuss is about, but does see the value in the collection – and in the charm of whisky paraphernalia, psychedelic carpets and a coin-operated pool table. All of which makes the Grouse a brilliant place to lurch into when the front tyre on my car bursts in a run-in with a pothole.

It must once again be said that whisky and being behind the wheel of a car do not mix, especially when that car has a blown-out tyre. So, joined eventually by my friends, the chances of halting at one whisky or arranging for my tyre to be fixed today are negligible. It is decided instead to try a few whiskies and then to work up an appetite by walking from here to the house where we're staying, an hour and a half's walk away – a stroll that the recently formed MWB, or Mad Walking Brigade, feel is very achievable – provided we've got a nip of something to keep us going. There is rumour of some slow-cooked beef that's been in the oven since the MWB left the house earlier in the day, and I don't have the heart to tell them about the beef pie I had for lunch, but we settle up, pocket whiskies fully charged, and head out into the darkening afternoon.

I am not a great country man. I own neither wellington boots nor walking boots, and I am here to tell you that robust trainers – in this instance a set of green leather Nike Air Force Ones – are no match for the undulations of a boggy Scottish walk. What I can attest to though is that Scotland is full of deer that can jump alarmingly high, and that when you stroll across open bogland with views for miles in every direction, it is a pleasure to watch the deer prance and leap in the distance. But there's more to the story than picturesque views across the bogs. The deer population in Scotland has doubled over the last thirty years; today nearly one million wild deer prance about the place, and without proper culling the population would grow further still. So what? That was my response, but the Scots are a little ahead of the rest of the UK and are trying to manage their environment with foresight. A rampant deer population would wreak havoc on attempts to grow sustainable forests, ripping up saplings which are so needed for biodiversity and to mitigate the effects of climate change. They destroy crops and livestock, too, not to mention the large number of road traffic accidents they cause each year on rural roads. And so there exists a perfect paradox. Killing deer seems cruel, yet keeping more deer alive seems foolish. One solution, which sounds quite exciting but terrifying, is to reintroduce once-native wolves and lynx back into Scotland as part of a larger programme of rewilding, which in turn would reduce the population to its natural level and no doubt add a certain type of biodiversity to the landscape. The other touted option is to eat more venison – a scenario in which landowners and farmers have a financial incentive to cull the deer, and the rest of us receive a healthy, lean, sustainable source of protein for those who are that way inclined. And we don't have to worry about wolves while on a walk, which is nice too.

It is with this lesson in mind, cobbled together as we walk through a combination of hearsay, local knowledge and internet research, that we arrive at our destination, a low white house in a horseshoe shape around a bonny little lawn – the only manmade structure for as far as the eye can see. I peel off my shoes and socks, light a fire (the first, and hopefully last, in my life using peat) and settle down to a very good beef stew, hearty with red wine and little pearl onions that have become rich, beefy bon bons in the cooking liquor. The stew might easily have been venison, but there's time for that; this was perfection too, served as it was with mashed root vegetables and a little more of the amber water. I'd earned my rest by then, and I retired for the night heavy with sleep and feeling, for the first time in my life, something like a countryside man.

The next morning, one of the Mad Walking Brigade was up early, and so coming downstairs I was presented with a Scottish breakfast. It was essentially something we'd all recognise, though there are a few key differences in fried breakfasts north of the border. You have all the usual favourites, of course – bacon, some fried mushrooms, beans if you must – but you'll often have a tattie scone in place of toast. They're similar to Irish farls – they're flat little breads made from a dough of potato, flour and water, and they taste wonderful with salted butter. Today they're in their element among all these other treats, none more exciting than the griddled lorne sausage that sits nonchalantly on my plate. For the uninitiated, the lorne sausage is a flat sausage made from ground beef, rusk and spices, a square version of the patty you'd find in a sausage and egg McMuffin. The rusk makes the thing moist and gives it a pleasing chew, and the spices bring a slight mystery to its flavour. There's always nutmeg, and plenty of pepper, a combination that is exotic and homely at the same time. And perhaps, in today's sausage, paprika and coriander too?

The breakfast savoured and the washing up done, I

sip my coffee and flick through a book I spotted on the kitchen shelf by Catherine Brown, simply titled *Scottish Cookery*. After yesterday's lessons in Highland deer, I turn immediately to the chapter on game. The section opens with a quote from 'a Highland Lady', talking up the bounty of 'plentiful red deer, roe, hares, grouse, ptarmigan and partridge; the river provided trout and salmon ... the garden abounded in common fruits and vegetables; cranberries and raspberries ran over the country'. This was the food of the people, and you could grow what you wanted and kill what you needed and live well, no matter your lot. It goes on to say that when Queen Victoria and Albert bought Balmoral in 1852, it became illegal to shoot or capture any game or wild fish. Perhaps it also explains the Scots' loyalty to the genre. More venison and game appears on menus up here than anywhere else in the country, and they cook it better too.

Fascinating as this history is, I am here for the recipes – to adopt the local knack for getting it right, to learn how to cook venison properly. And soon I land upon a set of rules that I can take away wholesale, hurrah.

Rule 1. The tender cuts – loin, tenderloin, chops and steaks – are best cooked hot and fast. Noted. Rule 2. The tougher cuts – head, feet, neck, shoulder, chuck and shank – are best cooked low and slow. Noted. Hold on, though, that's the same for every meat ever. I go back in. Marinades are good, and acidity helps weaken the muscle and make it more tender. Venison always needs a couple of hours in marinade. Sloe gin works well. As does port. I can feel gout coming on.

I have not lost all my enthusiasm for venison butchery and cooking, but I do have to press on with getting the tyre replaced and driving down towards Dunkeld, Perth, and then to Edinburgh and beyond.

I am but one man with one route, and as per my initial methodology I am travelling with practicality in mind. I am missing the Islands, the West Coast, perhaps even Glasgow and certainly much of the Borders, which means I am missing some of Scotland's finest food. But I am stopping indiscriminately where I can, eating from the cafés, restaurants and shops I pass along the way, and observing as the voyeur, making conversation like a nuisance when I can.

You'll be pleased to know that the tyre was fixed by a mobile mechanic with very little ceremony, and that he had with him cheese rolls wrapped in clingfilm and an Irn Bru for his lunch. I asked, he delivered.

And so, shoes dried, tyre replaced, knowledge of Scottish game improved, I head south again.

And before long, I am in Dunkeld. And then out of it, for Dunkeld is a relatively small place. While in it, though, I had time to note a few choice facts. One: it has a charming bridge that spans the River Tay, a beautiful body of water that makes you happy to be alive. Two: most buildings in Dunkeld seem to be painted a charming off-white, with subtle grey accents on the window frames, giving it the feeling of a Scottish (and slightly more staid) Santorini. This might be due to the fact that the day I stopped by it was bright and sunny and the River Tay was glistening like unfurled tin foil.

I'd decided to come off the A9 which connects the bottom of the Cairngorms with Perth; I'd heard rumours that Aran Bakery was a good spot to pick up some lunch, a loaf and some baked provisions on my journey. Aran Bakery is owned and operated by Flora Shedden, a baker, food writer and semi-finalist on the Great British Bake Off in 2015 – one of a growing band of enterprising young Scots keen to celebrate local produce, bring some proper hospitality and baking back to their local communities, and with a young, modern style that looks great both on social media and in person.

I buy a house sourdough and a perfect little rye bread, try an exemplary cardamom bun that almost fizzes with spice and a coffee that would rival any sold in a big city, and marvel at the quality of it all. I then walk up the high street and happen upon Dunkeld Fine Foods and Dunkeld Fish Bar.

Dunkeld Fine Foods is a tremendous establishment. Traditional-looking from the outside, with a touch of the health food store or the stuffy pine-clad 90s deli, it is only when you cross its threshold that the breadth and quality of its offering is revealed. All of Scotland's bounty is here; as long as you want oatcakes, great eggs, dairy and cheeses, premium local vegetables, good bread, great smoked, cured and potted fish products and extraordinary local meat and charcuterie, you can live very happily from this shop alone. It brings to mind the exceptional range this country has when it comes to producing smoked, preserved, cured and cooked meat and fish products, as well as the colossal breadth of British cheeses. I didn't buy any large chunks of cheese today, but the counter is strewn with samples of local treats that I couldn't resist as I browsed. I tried a rich, sweet Lanark blue that reminded me of Roquefort but with a slightly more manicured funk, and a St Andrew's Cheddar, twelve-month-aged, tangy and sweet. I liked the look of Black Crowdie, which turned out to be a soft cow's milk cheese, almost Boursin-like, that is rolled in pinhead oatmeal and ground black peppercorns. Before I leave I try a sample of Red Anster, a crumbly cheese with mild allium flavour, and Smoked Anster, a sweet and smoky delight. It seems a foregone conclusion that most towns will have a deli in which you'll find local and national cheeses and the like for your delectation. This wasn't always so.

Much like any country living off its land, Britain once had a much more vibrant culture of turning milk into cheese, preserving meats by salting and hanging, and doing the same with smoke or salt for fish. Add in chutneys, pickles, marmalades and jams and we had a preserving tradition that would have stood up to any in mainland Europe.

As with so many questions about why Britain is like this, the answer is: the Second World War. Rationing, which lasted until 1954, meant that small-scale artisan production was wiped out in favour of mass-produced, standardised food. The government even banned all soft and blue cheeses, and only 'scheduled' cheeses were allowed to be made, which included: Cheddar, Cheshire, Dunlop, Lancashire, Leicester, Derby, Wensleydale and Caerphilly – all of which was supplemented by the worryingly named 'Government Cheddar' that was shipped in from the US as part of their war aid. Which meant many producers who stopped making cheese during the war didn't go back into business afterwards, which in turn all but erased much of the country's regional cheesemaking heritage. By the time of the supermarket boom of the 1960s and 1970s, our traditional food culture had all but collapsed, while the likes of France, Spain and Italy continued to take immense pride in theirs.

A resistance was brewing, however, with a cabal of passionate underground revolutionaries working to revive what had been lost. British cheese was saved by the likes of Patrick Rance, whose 1982 *Great British Cheese Book* shone a light on the country's near-extinct farmhouse varieties, and Randolph Hodgson, whose Neal's Yard Dairy, founded in 1979 in London, bought whole production runs of small producers and cheesemaking farmers in order to create a viable market for raw milk cheeses. It's thanks to these foodie heroes that we've been able to preserve iconic names like Stichelton and Stilton, Montgomery's Cheddar and Stinking Bishop. The UK now has over 700 native or regional cheeses, which is more even than France. Hence the proliferation of delis on high streets, as here in Dunkeld.

Charcuterie, for its part, took a little longer to make a comeback. For years, British cured meats were seen as a joke compared to their European counterparts. But in the early 2000s, pioneering producers like the Weald Smokery, Trealy Farm and Cobble Lane Cured in London changed that, proving that air-dried ham, salami and chorizo made in Britain could rival anything from Spain or Italy. And while our own charcuterie culture certainly leans on France, Italy and Spain, places like the Weald Smokery have developed their own smoked chicken, duck and venison products that are uniquely British in style; they lean on meats native to us and hunted recreationally, while also relying less on fat or punchy spicing but instead elevating the flavour with a simple salt and sugar brine before carefully smoking it with native oak or fruit woods. All of which signals a culture that will continue to develop as our taste in charcuterie matures further.

Smoked fish never fully disappeared, however. Places such as the Inverawe Smokehouse near Oban, founded in 1974, helped preserve traditional oak-smoking techniques, while H. Forman & Son, the famous London smokehouse that produces wonderful smoked fish, revived the capital's historic smoked salmon industry in the 1990s. In 2017, London Cure Smoked Salmon even secured official protected status, joining the ranks of Champagne and Parma-made prosciutto as legally protected food products.

Scotland

All of which is to say, Dunkeld Fine Foods reflects this history perfectly, and this revival of our cured meat, cheese and fish industries is certainly an aspect of modern British cuisine that we can be particularly proud of – and an area that Scotland especially shines in.

All that said, the Dunkeld Fish Bar, for all that its fish and chips looks very good indeed, will now stand for ever in my mind as a business that represents an outdated view of Scottish food. I was about to order a cheeky battered haddock with which to make a little fish sandwich to eat down by the Tay, but approaching the counter I noticed a display offering the 'fried sweet of the day', today a deep-fried Bounty bar. I had an immediate visceral reaction, muttering 'the last thing Scottish food needs', before storming out.

Dunkeld now firmly in my rearview mirror, I was well on the way to the storied Horn Milk Bar.

The Horn Milk Bar is impossible to miss. There's a giant heifer on the roof, perfectly rendered in fibreglass and black and white paint. There's a Highland cow, all shaggy ginger fringe and cute horns, by the entrance, too, and a massive fibreglass strawberry by the fence. Inside, there's that specific stench of boiled meat, fried pork fat, burnt coffee and bleach that draws one in as much as it makes you heave. It reminds me of the heavy, hot, bleach-soaked cloths that my school lunch tables were washed down with, but also of a hotel breakfast buffet on a child-hood holiday. I take a pink upholstered seat at one of the Formica and wood laminate tables and immediately panic that I was meant to order at the counter; I stand up, then fall back as a woman waves me down.

'I'll be over, aye,' she says, 'unless you're rushing faster than the rest a' 'em?'

I have no idea if she means this in kindness or reproach, but I remain seated and resist taking out my phone or notebook as I feel the whole dining room is watching. I simply sit and smile, noting as I do the menu cards hanging above the counter.

I am here for a bacon sandwich – that was my instruction from Neil – but I note the milkshakes and decide on one too. Then the mince roll jumps out at me, and the chicken curry, and the bridie chips and beans too. And then I spot polony. I have no idea what bridie is, nor polony, and then the woman is back at my table.

'What can I get you?'

'Can I ask,' I start.

'No' in as much of a rush as you were, hey?'

I can't tell if she smiles or scowls.

'Bridie – can I ask what that is?' I am strongly conscious of my accent, assuming the minute I say it that I have pronounced 'bridie' wrong.

'Bridie,' she repeats back, ''s mince and onions in a foldover.'

She nods towards a table a few over.

'Oh nice, like a pasty?' I say, feeling pleased to have avoided any faux pas.

'No' like a pasty, no. Comes with chips and beans. Any else?'

Scotland

I almost don't ask, but I need to know what polony is.

'Polony? The roll. What is polony?'

'Pork sausage,' she says, scowling now, 'sliced and fried, or just sliced in a roll. Any else?'

'Can I please have,' I start, politeness my only solace now, 'a bacon sandwich …'

'Backstreakyoverdoneunder?' A word salad I cannot unpick.

'Brown sauce? And a milkshake.'

'The bacon. Back or streaky? Over or under done?'

'What do people tend to prefer?'

The look of disdain I receive only matches the feeling of shame that rises from my stomach to my throat like wet ink on blotting paper. What sort of lily southerner doesn't know how they like their own bacon? I can't bear to explain how I'm trying to carry out research.

'Streaky please, well done, and a bridie. And a chocolate milkshake. And a mince roll to take away.'

'Any fries?' I can't tell if she is mocking me.

'No thank you.'

I end up taking most of it back to the car. I must stress that everyone was very friendly in the Horn. I was just out of sync with the rest of the room. It was not the nice woman's fault, but it felt easier to be back in the car than sitting there making her day worse by being a bit weird every time she had to interact with me.

The Horn is a throwback, which is lovely and nostalgic, but it's throwing back in some ways to what many might see as a bleak time in our culinary past. To a time when our own traditions were only tenuously present, and we had adopted a lot of trends and processed foodstuffs from America into the void left behind after rationing and the loss of our own culinary traditions. The polony roll turned out to be what Americans refer to as baloney, which of course comes from Bologna, and which in Italy is known as mortadella. A finely minced pork (or beef and pork, in some places) sausage in a casing (synthetic red here and in the US, natural pig's bladder in Italy), it can be sliced and eaten as is, or fried and used in a sandwich. Bridie is very similar to a pasty or a meat pie and was 'invented' in Forfar in the 1850s. If it has one hole in the top it is simply beef; if it has two it is beef and onion. I am told the same is true of a Scotch pie. The mince in the mince roll is deliciously plain, heavily seasoned with something like Bisto, and moreish in a way that defies logic. It is still, I am led to believe, one of, if not the most popular meal in Scotland, with 30 per cent of the respondents in a *Scottish Daily Express* poll saying they eat it at least once a week. Some traditions do live on.

What's fascinating to me so far is that there's an unclear sense of what's new in Scottish cuisine. I've seen nirvana at the Anderson, but that's one man and his vision, and the bakeries are good, but has anything radically new come about in recent times? Have new communities in Scotland added to the national culinary conversation? Not that I have seen so far. And I guess the question is, does that matter? There is reinvention of long-held traditions when it comes to how game is viewed, and the makers showcased in Dunkeld suggest a food scene and an appetite for traditions given new life. As I head south to the bigger cities and beyond, I feel I have not yet found much forward-looking Scottish food.

Although everything I've seen so far has been a tradition, a tweak to tradition or a reinvention of one, I know Scotland is a forward-thinking country – it's the home of the tikka masala for god's sake – and ahead of me lie its most diverse cities: Edinburgh and Glasgow, which have growing populations that increasingly identify as being from an ethnic minority (19 per cent in Glasgow and 18 per cent in Edinburgh according to the 2022 census, and up from around 5 per cent in 2001). I also know that both have large South Asian populations, especially from India and Pakistan, and that growing Palestinian, Lebanese and Syrian communities have led to a wonderful rise in Levantine cuisine in both cities. This is on top of a lot of historic immigration to Scotland from Italy. The truth is, though, that 92 per cent of Scotland's population is White Scottish, and a further 4 per cent is recorded as Irish, British, Polish or 'other'. So to have given space and credence to so much wonderful food from other cultures is testament to Scotland's openness, and shows a forward-thinking country willing to embrace new cultures and cuisines with open arms while still preserving more of its traditional food culture than many other places in the UK.

In Edinburgh now, I gather my bearings and prepare for the next investigation in the Pear Tree pub, up by the university and around the corner from the Nile Valley Café, a student favourite serving Sudanese and Middle Eastern food since 1996. I was a student in Edinburgh myself, and this is the first time I have returned to the Nile Valley since I visited almost daily eighteen years ago. Back then I stuck religiously to the Bary Wrap, which combined falafel, shredded chicken, broad beans and hummus in a delicious homemade wrap, and was, from memory, no more than about three pounds fifty. It is still here, and it is only five fifty now. As I did then, I got my wrap to go and ate it in the pub around the corner. I wish I had known then that I was missing out on the offerings of tagines, Egyptian lamb molokhia, chicken wings, tabbouleh and fish curry.

I only have two days in the city and a list as long as my arm of places to try. So, notebook safely stowed, I head out to survey the roads back towards the city centre, down into New Town, out towards Leith and hopefully, if I have time, to coastal suburbs and villages beyond – Portobello, Gullane and Musselburgh.

In a place as vast as Edinburgh, it is impossible to stop and eat everywhere you want to, so my voyage of discovery inevitably ends up as more of a 'taking the temperature'. It is more about looking at menus, tallying the variety of places you come across, noting trends in cuisines, snooping in supermarkets to see what's on the shelves, what speciality shops exist on high streets, which cultures and cuisines are represented, which might be absent, what traditional dishes or foods are present, which dishes have disappeared or morphed or modernised – and how.

I find a groundswell of great Asian food. Kissa Orwell is a Japanese spot in an old police box in the west of the city; Leith Walk has some extraordinary Thai and Vietnamese places: a much-lauded spot called Mirin does amazing ramen among other plates of Asian-inspired treats. The Bami makes great Vietnamese sandwiches; there are Italian delis and restaurants galore, including the old trusty Valvona & Crolla. Once you're in Leith itself there are the extraordinary restaurants owned by Roberta Hall McCarron and her husband, who have a distinctive skill of combining the best of Scottish ingredients with modern European flavours and other influences. There are coffee shops and bakeries galore, notably Twelve Triangles, Beatnik and Lannan Bakery, the home of some of the most gorgeous pastries you'll ever see – and with a revolving menu that changes with the season. There's plenty of Indian and Chinese food, too, although I didn't find much in the way of Asian supermarkets (I'm told that's because the best ones are located in the surrounding suburbs of Edinburgh rather than in the city centre).

Edinburgh is one of Europe's largest financial centres, second only to London in the UK, and so it can sustain restaurants of every persuasion, price bracket and cuisine. You name it, it has it. And it has enough butchers, cheesemongers, fishmongers and delis to keep most people happy for a lifetime. What it doesn't seem to have is a big food market, the kind where traders tout their wares under tarpaulins or from makeshift huts or booths.

I take the train to Glasgow for the day and try a couple of great restaurants, Julie Lin's GaGa and a place called Gloriosa, one Malaysian, the other Mediterranean. And of course I make a beeline for Mother India, made famous by a visit from the late Anthony Bourdain, and by all accounts home to some of the best Indian food in Scotland. And during the course of all this wandering, I ate well. Edinburgh and Glasgow are both cities where food is important. The whole world is here, but as is true in many of the UK's largest cities, specificity of cuisine and nuance of place gets flattened by the hordes, by tourism, by the heft of a city that will eventually bend what you want to make and sell to its own whims. Whereas my time travelling from Cromarty to Edinburgh had me reflecting on Scotland's changing place in the British food landscape, I don't have the same sense upon leaving Edinburgh to drive to the North-East, my next stop. That is not to say I am not sated. It's just that Edinburgh – like Glasgow – has it all, which makes it harder to define a sense of what food in Edinburgh is. I finish my few days of tramping to every corner of Edinburgh in Kay's Bar in the Old Town. There's no food here, just good beer and the greatest room to drink it in of any I've found. Not too long, narrow enough, cosy from a red decor that somehow becomes a raucous backdrop when the mood in the room is right. You can drink in silence or find yourself in a male voice choir, both in the same night if you're lucky. And there's wonderful whisky. This feels like a fitting end to Edinburgh, and to Scotland; it is old-school, laden with tradition, but not stuffy. It's how I've found everything up here. Light-hearted about progress, accepting of the new, proud of tradition, with the new, the old and the radical existing all at the same time.

2

The North-East

To get from Edinburgh to the Northumberland coast, one can head down through the Borders, past Galashiels, Jedburgh and Hawick before hitting the top of the Northumberland National Park and turning left, aiming squarely for Alnwick, home to the biggest second-hand bookshop in the UK. Or one can go west, tracing the coastline from Portobello to North Berwick and Dunbar, then down along the rugged coastline and over the border to Berwick-upon-Tweed, Lindisfarne, Seahouses and eventually Alnwick. Both routes are spectacular, a joy to undertake. I ran a knitwear business in my twenties, and our factory was in Hawick. The water in the Borders is particularly good at keeping wool soft during the production process. As a result, there are plenty of knitwear businesses in the north-east, but – if memory serves – fewer iconic food businesses. The thought plays on my mind as I decide which direction to travel. Hawick is beautiful but a mite dull, so I find myself whipping along the coastal road, the sea on my left, a continuous film reel of British coastal highlights.

This is a gorgeous part of the world, with delights in every town – but I'm on a mission, and decisions must be made. I don't break off to North Berwick, but if I did, the beach at Milsey Bay, the tide out, would be reliably picturesque, the little matchbox houses at the edge of town rendered in pastel hues. This means I don't pass by Seaview either, a sandy beach with views to the Bass Rock that rival any from the Outer Hebrides to the Grand Canyon. I fly out towards Dunbar and whip past Broxburn, Cockburnspath and Eyemouth, liking, as I always do, the exuberance of the names. I see signs for Berwick-upon-Tweed, the northernmost town in England, and decide again not to stop. Had I pulled over, I would have likely ended up at A Corvi, an unassuming café that does very good-value fish and chips, which rival almost any others with fancier pretensions. Today is not a fish and chips day, and I'm keen to get down to Lindisfarne, where monks make mead, and beyond to Alnwick and then Tynemouth, where the best seafood restaurant in Britain operates out of a shipping container.

Before long I'm seeing signs for Haggerston and Beal, and soon enough for the Holy Island causeway. This means leaving the A1, and heading out over the sea on a slippery little causeway that only appears from beneath the waves at low tide, a treat on a sunny day when the slick sandflats reflect the sky and it feels like driving out across a mirror.

Lindisfarne, or the Holy Island, is a curious place

indeed – inevitable, I suppose, if you're cut off from the mainland most of the time. There has been a monastery or priory on Lindisfarne since long before the Vikings turned up here, but that's not why I'm here. I navigate the causeway with caution – although it looks dry today, I always feel like a careless slip is possible. I park in a field before heading towards the centre of this funny little place. As I walk I am surrounded by a near-equal split of earnest-looking late-middle-aged Brits in walking boots and Gore-Tex and tourists from all over the place, whether families with bored-looking children or earnest groups of history lovers. I first came to Lindisfarne as a child, and I have a distant memory of being mesmerised by piles of lobster pots adorned with faded once-neon nylon rope. And my memory suggests I might have tried my first oyster on the island; the Pavlovian trigger of being here certainly brings back to mind the shock at the sweet minerality of the snotty thing, and the excitement inherent in wanting more of something I'd assumed would be so disgusting. I certainly recall oyster beds, their structure looking like a miniature woodland, algae-covered cages sitting on rickety frames as you looked out from the headland. As I walk up into the centre of the village I see the Lindisfarne Mead headquarters and feel pleased with my decision to risk the tides. It's an uninspiring glass and wood-clad structure that looks like a visitor centre, but it holds bottle after bottle of the saccharine liquor that is made by fermenting honey, herbs and water. The mead they make here nowadays is more of a fortified wine, made from fermented honey, grape juice and spirits – and, I discover to my chagrin as I enter the Lindisfarne Mead headquarters, sweetened with other flavours such as strawberry, elderflower and cherry. It's not sacrilege to flavour mead like this; the old monks would have used whatever they found around the island – herbs, flowers, plants and even seaweed – but they'd be rolling in their cassocks at some of the flavour combinations. Never mind that the production of mead on the island has long been a folly, a marketing fad, a way to talk about an old British drink that has fallen from common consumption, but it was never the reason for my detour. My main reason for exploring the island is to head out past the castle and see the oyster beds before scoping out the town and finding a place that will sell me one or two to try. You're out in the North Sea here, not by much, but it's a beautiful spot for birds. I am no twitcher, but signs all about the place suggest a dizzying variety of geese, waders and the like that circle about the island, wheeling and screeching. I note in my little book the names of a few: grey plover (which I annotate with a grey pullover for my own amusement), bar-tailed godwit (which I still find a funny name), redshank, dunlin and purple sandpiper are common. One sign reports that this is a stopover point for birds migrating from Greenland to Africa, all of which explains the small stream of enthusiasts heading across the fields to the bird-watching station.

The North-East

Eventually I make it to the castle and stare out to sea, though I cannot see anything resembling the algae-covered forest I recall. I pull it up on my phone to check my childhood memory and the photo I find on the Lindisfarne Oyster company website looks exactly as I remember – the oyster beds must be out there somewhere. From the photos online, they cover an area of the seabed equivalent to a large field or two, and the locals have been farming oysters for nearly seven centuries. I walk up and down the coast a little, looking out to sea all the time, without success. Accepting defeat, I head back towards the town to see if I can find a seafood stall or a pile of lobster pots to satisfy at least one of my flights of nostalgia. A promising-looking stall beside the road seems to sell jams and other produce, so my expectations are high.

On the walk out to the castle I've clocked a post office, a pub and village store and a shack that I assume sells seafood. My plan is to start at the shack, before checking out the other two to see what British food looks like on little Lindisfarne. I have a hopeful feeling that it might just put many places in the UK to shame – but it's always the hope that kills you.

I found a crab sandwich. Actually, I found two crab sandwiches. And two more confusingly priced sandwiches I have never come across. The first came from the shack, labelled as a Holy Island fresh crab sandwich, and was priced at £4.50. The second was from the café attached to the local post office, also labelled as a Holy Island fresh crab sandwich, and was priced at £10.95. I bought the second because the first sandwich, the one from the shack, was underwhelming to say the least. I can only chalk up the price of the second to its use of flatbread and for an accompanying salad garnish that contained mostly thick ribbons of carrot. There's an art to making a crab sandwich – Holy Island or not – and while the brown meat of a crab is full of punchy crab flavour, it shouldn't have to do all the heavy lifting. Plenty of that sweet white meat is needed for balance, for levity and for luxury, things which were sadly lacking in both sandwiches. It was heartening to see local crab on the menu at Holy Island, though. Perhaps the crab salad I see on offer at the post office café would've done better justice to the humble crustaceans. When I see a plate land on a table in front of a gaggle of experienced walkers, all of them with cork-handled retractable walking poles and zip-kneed trousers, it's easy to see where the white crab meat on the island is ending up.

What is most disheartening, though, above even the fact that I haven't managed to find any Lindisfarne oysters, is that hot dogs, chilli dogs, bacon and Brie sandwiches, tuna melts and red pepper hummus seem to dominate every menu on Lindisfarne. The pub has a nice chalkboard full of tempting fishy dishes, but there is nothing especially local about the menu – and very little of the seafood that's caught or harvested locally seems to be on it.

As I trudge back to the car, a combination of disappointment and the sulphuric scent of sun-dried seaweed hastening my departure, I wonder why we so often ignore the bounty that's on our doorstep. Is it because restaurant kitchens fall into the trap of buying from one or two – often national – suppliers, whose stocklists tend to be generic, to keep the supply chain neat and tidy? Is it that places need neatly portioned, pre-packaged fish and seafood, perhaps bought frozen to reduce wastage, meaning that we end up excluding small local suppliers? Is it that customers just want burgers, pulled pork, simple sandwiches or soup? It's even more frustrating when pubs and restaurants make a gesture at offering something local, but don't buy local produce. Customers expect that a pub on the coast should sell fish, so there is fish on the menu, but relying on the fresh local catch would be more expensive than seeing what's in the walk-in at the normal supplier. Is it the constant fear of not making ends meet, or something else? I don't know.

What I do know is that on a tourist-filled island with a centuries-long history of monks, mead, birdlife and seafood, only the birds seem to be properly present. The mead has been commodified and ruined with faux-medieval branding, and although the seafood is still out there in the water, it's not on the menus in any meaningful way.

As I carry on down the coast, headed towards Tynemouth and Riley's seafood shack, I find myself feeling increasingly evangelical about how crucial places like Riley's are in showcasing the seafood from our own waters, how to cook it and charge a price that reflects its splendour while not precluding all but the most affluent from trying it.

I haven't arrived yet, and part of my brain is occupied by the inevitable hustle for a parking space on Sea Banks, the road that runs above the cove where Riley's is nestled. The rest of my brain is running through what I've previously eaten at Riley's, trying to escape the disappointment of the crab sandwiches. The ever-present mackerel wrap, its skin salty and blistered and smoky from the grill, the griddled bread salty and soft, some samphire, a signature fennel salad, the potatoes – oh the potatoes – and a zingy herb sauce. Or the piece of halibut as thick as a book, its skin brittle, the fish itself pristine, a mayonnaise tasting robustly of olive oil but of lemon, too. Or – wait, there's more – a special dish, something for celebrations, a whole turbot in a bisque thick with brown crab meat, and mussels too, and samphire probably, with bread for mopping up so that no bisque goes to waste. I could go on. I've reached the clifftop parade at Tynemouth now, and a Nissan Micra is fortuitously reversing out of a space in front of me. My indicators are on and I sit blithely in the road, the honks of traffic insignificant as I'm wrapped in my reverie. Seafood Valhalla awaits and, after the morning's deflating diversion, it cannot come soon enough.

Riley's take reservations now, a fact I was not aware

of, but a fact that you, dear reader, should make the most of. I join a short queue of other coves who also didn't realise you can book, and before too long I am sitting proudly on a stool at a raised bar, my vista nothing but breaking waves and frolicking Brits on blue deckchairs or hunched behind navy windbreakers. Many are sitting on the sand with a glass in their hand and a small bamboo plate or two propped on their knee. For these are not just beach dwellers, these are my fellow diners, and for the price of a mackerel wrap or a crab soufflé they are enjoying an experience normally reserved for honeymooners in the Maldives or bronzed families in the Caribbean.

Riley's started life as a street food stall at a food market in Newcastle in 2012. Adam Riley was a theatre set designer who decided to start selling seafood wraps from a bicycle to celebrate the local fish and seafood that was not available to many Geordies. It's fair to say the stall was popular; the now-signature queues were an immediate occurrence. Before long Adam and his wife Lucy were seeking planning permission for a commercial shipping container on a picturesque local beach, King Edward's Bay, and they've been full ever since. So far, so charming, but what makes it so special? Well, the other notable seafood institution in Tynemouth is the North Shields Fish Quay, a Monday-to-Friday year-round fish auction that sells catch from day boats operating out of North Shields. This is where Riley's buy their fish, every morning. North Shields is the busiest fishing port on the east coast of England. While Scarborough, Whitby, Grimsby and Hull have lost almost all their fleets, North Shields continues to flourish. Alongside a hundred or so visiting trawlers from places such as Ireland, Scotland, the Netherlands and Denmark, thirty local day boats operate out of the port throughout the year – and the bulk of that catch passes through the daily auction.

So when Riley's buy from the auction, they're buying the freshest catch at the best price, but they can plan a menu that will perfectly reflect the changing seasons of the sea while showcasing what is sustainable and abundant. And if the produce was only landed that morning and goes straight on to the menu that lunchtime and evening, all the food will be at its freshest and best. To boot, much of what is purchased by Riley's is incidental catch from scampi boats. These are often species that are less in demand, which means they are less targeted by the commercial boats, and so using them puts less stress on the local ecosystem while supporting the local fishermen by purchasing more of their catch. Win win.

All that remains then is for the team at Riley's to cook the fish perfectly, which they do, and to serve it with accompaniments designed to complement the main event without stealing focus – though the fact that their potatoes are a highlight is a testament to the simple, skilful cooking here. It always strikes me that supreme fish cookery is about having a dearth of ego, about making sure the fish is the star. For a business as phenomenally successful as Riley's, there is pleasingly little hyperbole online. I know that Rick Stein has given the place his seal of approval, and Vice came up this way to make a video in 2017, but that's about it. Since then Riley's has only got busier; they've opened a fish shop too, where you can purchase the same fish that Riley's use on their menu while stopping for lunch or dinner. And it's as busy today, a midweek afternoon, as it's been any time I've visited.

This was not meant to be a review of Riley's, nor a sermon on the place, but after my frustrations at Lindisfarne, and from my myriad encounters with mediocre food across the country, it's exhilarating to know of a business doing something so fantastic with British fish and seafood, which should be our pride and joy. That places like Riley's are rare lends to the feeling of frustration. Three Lindisfarne oysters are quickly in my palm, as is a plate of the aforementioned brown crab soufflé, both stupendous – the oysters for their clean minerality, the soufflé for being anything but. Then, for old time's sake, a monkfish wrap, the meaty fish carrying smoky char from the grill, the sourdough flatbread pillowy and covered with aïoli and coarse salsa verde. It is one of the best fish dishes I've ever tasted, brought together into a perfect mouthful with some of the famous potatoes, shaved fennel with lime salad and some fresh jalapeños and mint. It is no wonder the dish remains the number one seller at Riley's after twelve years.

For just over £50, I've had a three-course meal of

some of the best fish and seafood I've ever tasted. That the crab soufflé is only a couple of pounds more expensive than the crab sandwich I forced myself to eat earlier in the day is baffling, and says something interesting about food in this country. Both the sandwich and the soufflé needed a person to take a collection of raw ingredients and fashion them into a dish for someone to eat. When costing each of them, the cook's wages are a large percentage; the crab probably about the same cost for both, with the remaining bits and pieces being the biggest point of difference. The fact that the soufflé was mind-bendingly good and the sandwich was hard to stomach is simply down to one person wanting to make something as delicious as possible and the other executing a thing because punters expected to see it on a menu. The crab salad I saw the group of walkers tucking into was £16.95; for £16 at Riley's I could have chosen between grilled squid with roast aubergine caponata, lemon sole meunière, squid ragù with polenta and slip sole with spring veg, wild leeks, garlic and seaweed butter.

This leads me on to my final fascination with places like Riley's. When a food business is that busy for that long, you'll get an instinctive sense of what your customers like and what they don't. Alongside the fresh-as-can-be locally caught seafood on the menu at Riley's, we have: empanadas, aïoli, harissa, caponata, meunière, Café de Paris butter, pav bhaji, raita, sumac and pistou. None of these are British by origin, but most of them will be recognisable to a keen British diner. Here is a menu that reflects what British food is right now to Adam, Lucy and the chefs at Riley's – but also to the diners, as this is what they are responding to, ordering in their droves. We want diversity, we want bright flavours on a cold day, and so influences from across the Med, the Middle East and India coexist on the menu of a fish shack in North Shields where people queue for hours along the sea wall. Local, seasonal, not afraid to try out new flavours. It's a vision of British food I can get behind.

The time has come to head to Middlesbrough – and if I've developed a sense that we've untethered ourselves from traditional British dishes without replacing them with something embedded in local culture, the parmo stands as a monument against that argument. It's the opposite of Riley's. I hope it's not overstating things to suggest that a certain stratum of Middlesbrough's identity has been built on this breaded escalope since it was introduced to the city in the late 1950s.

I know I'm approaching Middlesbrough not because I'm crossing the River Tees, nor because of the faint industrial tang in the air, but because I spot someone levering a fluorescent piece of breaded meat, bathed in béchamel and melted Cheddar, towards their face from a pizza box as I pass in the car. This is a parmo, it is what I am here for, and it is as Middlesbrough as the Riverside Stadium and the Transporter Bridge.

The parmo's origin story has become local legend, a culinary fable. Invented by Nicos Harris, a Greek Cypriot chef who served in the British Navy during the Second World War before settling in Teesside in the 1950s, it was first cooked at the American Grill on Linthorpe Road. The parmo is inspired by the Italian-American parmigiana, but reinterpreted through the lens of post-war British palates and with many of the key ingredients switched for what was available in Middlesborough at the time. The aubergine was out, the tomato sauce too messy, mozzarella too foreign. Instead: deep-fried breaded pork cutlet (later, more commonly chicken), rich béchamel, Cheddar cheese, with the whole thing whacked under the grill until bubbling and bronzed. The parmo was born.

If Riley's Fish Shack is an ode to restraint and seasonality, the parmo is the opposite: loud, brash and excessive, but no less deeply beloved. It's not trying to be elegant. It's trying to fill you up, make you feel better, and remind you exactly where you are. And in Middlesbrough, that's everything.

Like any dish with a hold over a place, it has become more than just food. It is ritual, it is identity, it is post-match, pre-hangover, end-of-the-night comfort. Takeaways like Uno Momento, Parmo King and Manjaros have each developed a cult following and fierce local loyalties, with some offering parmo menus longer than a French wine list. You can have your parmo classic (chicken, béchamel and Cheddar), or jazzed up with garlic mushrooms, hotshot peppers, doner meat, pepperoni or pineapple. There are vegan versions. There is a chocolate parmo. There are parmo pizzas. There are parmo challenges where you are dared to eat one the size of a road sign. There are parmo awards. Parmo crawls. Parmo-flavoured crisps. Parmo wedding buffets. Parmo tattoos.

And so, at just gone half eight and with the daylight fading, the good people of Middlesbrough are starting to fill the streets in all their finery, showing signs of making a pretty decent night of it if the noise levels and the tightly gripped bottles and cans are anything to go by. The gaudy neon signs of the shops along Linthorpe Road are flickering into life, their siren call immediately effective. I've singled out a highly regarded spot for my maiden parmo: parked on a side street just off Linthorpe Road, we're a stone's throw from where the parmo was invented. There are plenty of options, but I've decided that my spot will be Manjaro Express, the smaller sibling to the flagship Manjaro just up the road. It's sleeker than I suspected from the outside, all black-pleather banquettes and dark wooden floorboards. I hadn't expected to be sitting down; in fact, I'd envisaged inhaling the thing in the car. What a treat.

Inside now, there's a guy in a Middlesbrough shirt waiting for his order, which gives me the confidence to place my own. I am intimidated. That is worth stating here. The internet is ripe with lore when it comes to parmo, and passions run high. I feel in a state of near panic, lest I get my order wrong and offend someone. In front of me, a teenage couple hover over the menu. As I wait my turn, a man enters in paint-splattered jeans, his eyes red with the focus of someone for whom this parmo is not just a treat but a necessity, his only option to steady himself after a tiring day.

I stand in front of the counter, terrified by the myriad options; the warm bready fog of the fryer, the sweet undertow of bubbling béchamel and the full-fat comfort of melted cheese is intoxicating, even when sober. I have a sudden clarity of mind and order the classic chicken parmesan. Chips. Blue Fanta, the one that replaced Lilt. Garlic sauce.

And then I wait for ten minutes or so, long enough to watch the ballet behind the counter. The breadcrumbed fillets are lowered into hot oil to cook them most of the way. Then a thick béchamel is ladled and spread thick on to the golden crust of the hot parmo. This gets a blast under the hot grill and comes out bubbling and freckled before cheese is scattered in generous handfuls to cover the sauce. Then it goes under the grill once more to achieve that all-important surface burn. And then out it comes.

I collect my bounty, consider sitting in, but think better of it and return to the car. I peel open the box, and the car fills with the scent of fried cheese. It is not unpleasant, but neither is it something I'd want to stick around for too long. I wind down a window. The top of the parmo is almost comically perfectly bronzed and bubbling, the edges of the chicken crisp where they've escaped their duvet of béchamel. I have a knife and fork in the takeaway bag, and I've seen a video where cutting the parmo into manageable chunks seems like a good idea. I carve away at one corner. And then, the first bite. The breaded chicken still has crunch despite straining under its melted load, the béchamel is thick and smooth, and the cheese is doing everything it should. It's not just melted, it's cooked. The chips are chunkier than I might have imagined. They serve as both ballast and sponge, an unexpectedly useful combination. And the garlic sauce is more than a condiment; it's the supporting act this whole production depends on.

Drunk, this would be a game changer. You'd wake up more sober than when you started. Sober as I am, though, it's a different thing. There's no dulled sense of taste to hide behind. I can feel every gram of cheese, every twist of salt, every crunch. But it more than holds up. It shines. There's something deeply comforting in its excess. Not messy, but crafted. It reminds me of a shockingly stacked and gravied Portuguese Francesinha sandwich. A visual spectacle that you think will be too dense, too rich. And then it isn't, it's somehow balanced and pleasing and even moreish. So too, it turns out, is the parmo. Or a good parmo at least, one fried and grilled to perfection, burnished just so.

I can't help but admire the decadence. It tastes not of nostalgia, but of now. Of someone, somewhere, doing this dish right. And in Manjaros you can see the past, the present and the future of Middlesbrough, all through the parmo. Be it Italian, Indian, Caribbean or Cajun, there is a parmo out there that caters to every taste.

I manage a respectable half of the steering-wheel-sized treat. Sat with the windows down to allow the cheese smell to seep out of the car, I watch as a fox drags a crushed box from under a wheelie bin, noses open its lid and snaffles the ends of what looks like a Bolognese parmo. It scampers a few metres up the road, before flinging its head back, tossing the parmo into the air and catching it clean in its mouth. I have this noted in my little yellow book, so I'm pretty sure it happened; reading it back, I wonder if I might have been hallucinating from the cheese.

Leaving the windows down, I turn on the engine and beat my retreat from Middlesbrough, aiming to stop near Scarborough before exploring North Yorkshire tomorrow. As I drive out of town, I can't help but consider what food here used to be before parmo made its molten debut. Well, you might be unsurprised to hear that the story of food on Teesside could apply to most of the rest of the country.

Middlesborough was a steel town, a graft town. Food was fuel. Wartime rationing ended only in 1954, and the food culture reflected that: stews, boiled potatoes, tinned vegetables, suet puddings, Spam. There was corned beef – plenty of it, usually mashed with onion and potato into pies. Brown sauce, vinegar, and cups of tea so strong that they could stand a spoon up. Meat and two veg, lard-based pastries, tinned peaches with evaporated milk if you were lucky. A plate of tripe for the brave. All things you might have distant memories of, or might have heard your grandparents speak of fondly. In terms of buying food while out and about, fish and chips reigned supreme, as did pork pies and stotties (a type of bread roll from the north-east) from the local baker. There was nothing fancy, nothing flamboyant. Portions were solid. Seasoning was minimal. Italian, Greek, Caribbean, South Asian cuisines? Practically non-existent. The Boro palate of the 1950s was starchy, salty and sensible. And it's this culinary monochrome that made the arrival of the parmo so remarkable. In a town that had never asked for béchamel, someone served it, and it stuck. A European chef, cooking an Americanised version of an Italian dish, in a British industrial town, managed to create one of the UK's most regionally loved late-night foods. That's Middlesbrough magic, but it also might be Middlesbrough's albatross. This thing so obsessively filled the gap for flavour that for decades nothing else could gain enough traction to survive, so stultifying was the dominance of the parmo on the local cuisine. And we see this elsewhere too, be it with orange chips, spice bags or a particular kebab, pizza or snack; there was a gulf in the wake of rationing that often one or two dishes, or one or two cuisines, were able to fill depending on regional preference – and these things stuck. It is why only now, sixty years after rationing, we are truly starting to explore the true breadth and depth of the cuisines we've loved for so many years.

Of course, I am oversimplifying, Middlesbrough has moved on. The town's food landscape is no longer dominated solely by the parmo, even if it looms large still. Over the past two decades, a new generation of diners has demanded more, and the town has risen to meet it.

Teesside's growing Turkish and Kurdish communities have been taken into the fold, and it is not hard to find spots serving up regional treats, grilled meats and fluffy bread fresh from the oven. I pass Syrian falafel shops, Polish delis, Punjabi curry houses, proper Neapolitan pizza, and I'm told that if only I'd taken a minute to pause in Manjaros, it serves some of the best jerk chicken in the north-east. The monthly Orange Pip Market brings in a mix of independent food trucks, bakers and bao bun specialists. The beer scene is catching up too, with craft brewers and micro pubs starting up in disused garages and shops. There is a vitality here now, and variety, and while the parmo still sits on the throne, it is surrounded by a vibrant court of supporting players. Middlesbrough might be the only place in Britain where you can get a Caribbean parmo, wash it down with small batch Polish lager and have Syrian karabij for dessert – all from neighbouring spots on the same street.

The North-East

While Middlesbrough might not be a food city in the same way that London and Glasgow are, it is a place that might reflect even better than the big cities what British food is now, and where it is headed. Unlike so many places where regional dishes vanish under the weight of gentrification, Middlesbrough has managed to embrace new ideas without letting go of its heart – the parmo. And frankly, this is a cultural balancing act worth celebrating.

3

Yorkshire

Although I'd left half a parmo in Middlesbrough, the smell of cooked cheese was still in the car with me as I raced to Scarborough with the windows down. Scarborough is my gateway into Yorkshire, and the place from which I will head inland towards Ganthorpe, then York, before heading down to Ilkley, into Leeds and across to Bradford. It's an itinerary that I hope will bring into sharp focus the shifting demographics of the area – and how that's affected British food.

    I am charmed by Scarborough, in a way that one tends to be charmed by the faded grandeur of former spa towns or Victorian holiday resorts. Scarborough was both, and its origin story is familiar the country over. A medieval fishing port, the discovery of medicinal spring waters turned the place into a spa town in the seventeenth century. Once the Victorians started building grand hotels and connecting places with railways, suddenly there were pleasure gardens, music halls, new beaches and a pier – and by the late 1800s any Victorian worth their salt was coming up for their holidays. After the war, Scarborough remained a place to come to in the summer for scenic drives, to ride donkeys on the beach and throw coconuts at a shy. From then, it was all downhill. The 1970s brought foreign air travel to the masses, and pretty soon donkey rides with Grandpa and fancy sandcastles lost their allure, families stopped coming, deciding that Greece, Portugal or southern Spain were a safer bet. So the family stops coming, but Grandpa still loves the place, so he retires here, and so do all his friends; the quality of life is nice, but Scarborough is increasingly full of retirees and the grand hotels have lost their sheen. The old swimming baths have closed, and the arcades are empty.

Except that's not quite the full picture. Scarborough seems to have a little mojo left, or has found some new energy. There are families here, the promenade is busy and there's enough life in the place to sustain a few good coffee shops and the like.

Scarborough has an ageing population that is 97 per cent white. Between 2011 and 2021, the inhabitants aged between sixty-five and seventy-four increased by 21 per cent, while the number of people between thirty-five and forty-nine decreased by 17 per cent. So, I'm not expecting Scarborough to be a utopia in which I'll discover the new frontier of British food. The main drag along the beachfront is a repeating pattern of arcade, ice cream shop, doughnut stand and fish and chip shop. Among all this is the Harbour Bar, or Alonzi's as some know it, a typical old-fashioned ice cream parlour dolled up in Fifties Americana and serving coupes and shakes and splits and sodas as if D-Day was in the recent past and the GIs were still stealing our girls. It offers a charming hit of nostalgia. Alonzi's is busy, even midweek, but it tells me nothing about what British food is now – it exists only in the past.

And so, hungry for something savoury before I order an inevitable knickerbocker glory, I grab a 'lobster' baguette, some picked crab and a portion of chips from the highest-rated chip shop on the promenade and head on to the beach. Now, the ire I'm about to spew is derived from my knowledge that Scarborough, while no longer the powerhouse fishing port it once was, maintains a busy shellfish industry, with crab and lobster especially popular. I've bought seafood from kiosks up and down the country over the course of this trip, and raised as I was near the Kent coast, little pots of prawns, mussels, cockles, pickled rollmops and the like have long been a core part of my seaside picnic lexicon. The quality of this seafood is generally high, and whether as part of a bigger spread or for a life-affirming snack, nothing beats fresh seafood in a Styrofoam pot. Yet, when the quality isn't good, it suddenly casts British seafood in a bleak light. In most countries with coastlines, whether Sri Lanka, Indonesia, Mexico, or Portugal, Spain or Greece, there is a reverence for seafood that borders on the maniacal. Take enough of an interest, and you'll soon be inducted into a cult of local recipes that will have you taking to the seas, in love with the possibilities offered by the ocean's bounty. But what, instead, do *we* do with our fish, more often than not? Batter it, for one, or slather it in a cloying mayonnaise-based sauce such as a Marie Rose. We might smoke or cure it, but that's basically it. Our fishing stocks are among the world's best, and we haven't bothered to come up with much beyond batter, slather or smoke. And, considering the amount we've borrowed and plundered from cuisines abroad – take Indian or Cantonese food as the obvious examples – it's not as if we've taken the opportunity to do something delicious with our fabulous produce. Nope, we offer, at most, a prawn dish – and even then the prawns might have been frozen and imported from Thailand or Argentina. A lot of column inches since the Brexit referendum in 2016 have been dedicated to our beloved fishing industry, but on today's evidence it seems like we hate what they catch. This 'lobster' baguette is probably made with frozen crayfish, and my picked crab tastes slightly rancid, so long has it been kept sweating in the clingfilm-topped cup. Later, as I sit in the Harbour Bar, a banana split and a knickerbocker glory on the table in front of me and the rhythmic slopping of the ice cream mixture in the big metal churners soothing my mood, I wonder: why in every other realm of our British menu do we let the outside in, do we pinch and borrow from other cultures, finesse and reinvent dishes that were created far away, but when it comes to the fish section, we make no effort at all? Coronation chicken sandwiches (a few of which I have inhaled in service stations on this journey) have taken a Raj-era spice blend and turned it into a perennial British classic. Later, in Bradford, I'll be presented with a vision of what truly inventive cooking with fish could look like. I love the little shrimp fritters that you find in Kerala and Sri Lanka. Lightly spiced and fried with onion in a crunchy batter, they couldn't be more addictive if they tried. I could go cuisine by cuisine, listing diaspora communities in the UK and their ways with seafood that would bring joy to a seaside menu board, but no, we get clingfilm-wrapped baguettes with sweaty, mayo-heavy blandness. More fool us.

I liked Scarborough a lot, and don't want to single the place itself out as being particularly heinous. Still, it feels nice to leave behind the sickly-sweet nostalgia hit of the old British seaside and to be heading to Ganthorpe and nearby Malton, the newly crowned foodie capital of the UK. Now, I know I said I wouldn't be actively seeking foodie hotspots, but this one is by chance; Ganthorpe is a convenient stopping point, and only once I'd checked into a charming holiday cottage there was I told about Malton's credentials.

Malton is situated to the east of Castle Howard and the Howardian Hills, which makes this a rarefied, perhaps even regal, landscape. Castle Howard itself is a Baroque house with a massive estate, which was used as the filming location for recent adaptations of *Brideshead Revisited*. It has not only a gift shop but an on-site butcher and delicatessen, placing it firmly in the 'useful big old houses' category if you're passing. If you do happen to be nearby, though, don't feel bad about swerving Castle Howard and heading instead to Malton, a market town a few miles east which, for my money, is the platonic ideal of a good food town. Hearing a place has been anointed a 'foodie capital' might bring to mind greengrocers filled to the brim with glistening tomatoes, maybe something enticing and unpronounceable from South East Asia or an under-explored region of Italy. You might expect butchers and fishmongers, displays of choice cuts and pieces presented at their very best. And all this would, of course, come at prices that'd make you wish you'd swallowed your pride and done a shop in your nearest supermarket before arriving.

Well, not in Malton, my friends. Yes, Malton has all the constituent parts that could make this a nauseating place, but they're here to serve the community – not because a Swiss gallery owner wants you to come for a long weekend and realises you won't do so without a certain level of deli-led food shopping. No, Malton is for the Maltese.

Now, I am reliably informed that people from Malton are not known as Maltese. They are known to be discerning, though, and their discernment has allowed, encouraged even, a perfectly balanced food ecosystem to develop and thrive. So how does that look in reality?

Well, in the market square, Paley's is a greengrocer where the prices are more likely to make you say 'Cor blimey' than 'How much?!' Outside are barrows full of all the good stuff – apples, pears, big bags of potatoes, a few boxes of courgettes, carrots and cauliflowers – that have clearly been dug up and dropped off by someone with a smallholding as opposed to a solar-powered combine harvester. Inside there are tables laden with punnets of whatever's in season. You end up with a basket full of brown paper bags, your wallet lighter but not empty. Across the market square, you can find Derek Fox, a butcher specialising in game and poultry, and a fishmonger, Malton Fisheries, who do a good line in herrings and kippers. Add to this a couple of old-school bakeries of the steak bake, cream slice and granary loaf variety, and a Sainsbury's that hasn't had an upgrade since the late 1980s, and you have the perfect town for daily provisioning. And so I provisioned. And that evening, making the most of the holiday cottage's well-appointed kitchen, some fine herrings were dusted in flour, pan-fried and served alongside boiled potatoes and some good local greens. I used a lemon to give the whole thing a lift, but besides that everything was from here, and not at all piously presented.

If the produce on offer in Malton could be replicated up and down Britain, British food would be better, more varied and our choices would be supporting local business, not least because in any cuisine, the dishes cooked and eventually codified as being from that place are simply the result of local things being brought together in unique and delicious ways. Regional variety in dishes can only exist where there is regional variety in produce, and when the majority of the country buys its food from supermarkets it's not surprising that few of us can support local, seasonal offerings. That said, if everywhere was like Malton we'd lose much of the variety of cuisines that derive from the British magpie nature. So perhaps you can't have everything.

All good things must come to an end, and I'm meeting two of my culinary heroes just outside Leeds tomorrow. So I get back into the car and head to York, then on to Ilkley.

The truth is, I'm feeling overwhelmed by my food-based emotions. Driving around Yorkshire, it is hard to imagine a more English landscape. The bright green hillocks, the dry-stone walls, the thickets on yonder hump, it affects you, makes you feel that anything less than this is less than British. So do the thousands of sheep, all chomping at the ground and frolicking on verdant rises. And there's little arable farmland I can see, so lamb, onions, potatoes and carrots start to seem like the only thing that makes sense to eat. And lunch, unavoidably, will be some combination of that lot, wrapped in pastry or trussed up into a pie. And if not, then a local cheese, crumbled in with some piccalilli and a leaf or two of a market gardener's lettuce. Add a breakfast of some kippers or some devilled kidneys on toast with an egg and I start to see why a traditional British diet makes sense in a landscape like this. It sounds like an old-fashioned way of eating. Hardly anyone eats like that nowadays, I'm sure, but I haven't yet been grasped by any landscape I've been through in this way; I've come over all Jane Eyre and I can't seem to shake it.

York comes and goes. I'd skip it if I were you. I park in a side street right up against the old city walls, and am immediately fleeced for over twenty pounds for a couple of slices of quiche and two cans of ethical soft drinks in an establishment that seems to have stolen its menu from a health food shop in early 2000s Islington, and its prices from the hipster bakery that subsequently inherited the site in 2022. Desolate, I head for the centre of town, passing identikit chicken and pizza shops, then a mishmash of Harry Potter merchandise shops and high-street lifestyle shops that sell pots of smelly stuff with joss sticks poking out of them. Once in the market, my spirits are briefly lifted by a veg stall similar to my new favourite greengrocer's in Malton and a fishmonger with a nice display of kippers and smoked cod's roe. But the rest of the market is all smash burger concepts and doughy cookies. There are more stalls selling carved wooden ornaments or felt hats that an arty aunt might don for a winter walk than food. I always feel sad when I see a cynical food market, for they've chosen to sell tempting, high-margin items to tourists. If I see a crêpe stall, or a place offering chocolate-covered strawberries, I come over all melancholy. I'm sure there are producers and makers in York who sell wares that reflect the place, their own heritage and passions. Filling a market with such traders would create a wonderful place to shop and eat, and York would be better for it.

As it is, I'm back in the car well before my two-hour parking ticket expires and it's only when I go to type in my next destination on my phone that I notice the name of the market in York is 'Shambles'. It felt like being in Camden Town on a Saturday – and that's not a feeling I relish. I leave York behind and press on to Ilkley, through ever more arcadian landscape, hopeful that its proximity to Leeds and Bradford in the east and Skipton and Swaledale in the west will deliver something that's creative, original and delicious.

For its part, Ilkley is charming. Another spa town – and one that lured Charles Darwin, no less – it sits at the southern tip of the Yorkshire Dales and its surrounding countryside is straight out of central casting for a green and pleasant land. If the countryside around Castle Howard had me yearning for lamb hotpot, Ilkley could have me eating grey chops and over-boiled potatoes every night for a lifetime without minding too much, so long as I woke up every morning to that view. This feeling is not in any way softened when the directions from my Airbnb tell me to turn left after Bettys Tea Room, a Northern institution that feels old-fashioned but is one of Ilkley's seven wonders.

I've chosen Ilkley as a base so that I can take the temperature of Leeds and Bradford, both just a few miles away, but also because my two culinary heroes live and work in nearby Skipton. I've arranged to see Jorge Thomas, founder of one of the country's best whole animal butchers, and George Ryle, my old sous chef and one of the most naturally skilful cooks in Britain. Even without Bettys Tea Room, Ilkley couldn't be a more charming place to stop for a few days, especially if you have time for a ramble in the Rombalds, which might sound like a boxing prize-fight but is actually the name of the moors that surround the place. Ilkley was voted as the nicest place in the UK to live by the *Sunday Times* a few years ago, and if you're after a peaceful life within shouting distance of a major city, I'd say I concur. Sadly for me, I won't be getting out on the moors today. Instead, I'll start my ramble at the top of the town in Booths, the poshest of all northern supermarkets.

For those who haven't had the pleasure, Booths is much like Waitrose, in that it is owned by its members, proud of the breadth and quality of its offering, and a very pleasant if lip-puckeringly expensive place to shop. Booths supermarkets exist only in the North, a fact that many put down to links to local suppliers and communities, and the difficulty in developing them in new territories. They are largely found around Lancashire and the Lake District, but also in Cumbria and Yorkshire, with a solitary Cheshire outpost in Knutsford.

Booths was founded by Edwin Henry Booth, a nineteen-year-old orphan who was working as a tea dealer when he founded a store, the China House, in Blackpool. Once licensing laws were relaxed, the tea shop became a de facto off-licence; more and more shops were opened, and the stock was expanded to the breadth I find before me today. Always on the beat, I note vegetables that range from the brown-bagged and local to the imported and exotic. The Booths bakery is a thing of wonder, and there is no surprise that its range of teas and coffees is of great quality too.

I have to say that apart from an occasional heart palpitation when glancing at the price of something tempting but unnecessary, I'm enjoying my time in Booths. That is, until I come to the dry goods aisle and am confronted by the tiny range of spices. Aside from what I would consider entry-level herbs and spices from the 1990s – cumin, five-spice and a few mixed dried herbs – there was nothing of interest. There were none of the usual Middle Eastern treats such as sumac and za'atar, nothing god-tier such as Szechuan peppercorns, black cardamom, asafoetida or even a smoked salt or niche dried chilli such as the nice long arbol or smoky little ancho. I searched and searched, but couldn't even find a normal dried chilli. Smoked paprika had to do.

I bought a decent bagful of groceries and returned to my accommodation, taking note as I did so of the rest of the offering in Ilkley. There is a pleasing simplicity to its high street – especially for someone who grew up in the Surrey commuter belt. There is a common-or-garden Chinese takeaway, the celebrated Bettys

Tea Room, a couple of coffee shops, one trendier and one more likely to draw in the local WI crowd, and a bakery, of course. As for dining out, there are six or seven Italian restaurants ranging from the entry-level place with a big pepper grinder and cheeky waiter, to the more salubrious white-tablecloth-and-a-big-Barolo, a French bistro called Chez something, a couple of brunch spots, a Thai restaurant, three Indian places, at least one kebab shop and a good few pubs.

Walking in circles around Ilkley as I noted all this down, I had plenty of time to consider the offering in Booths; by the time I was back at my accommodation, I went straight on to their website to check a few of my knee-jerk takeaways. I immediately landed on their recipe page. The Booths recipe archive is a fairly predictable offering, but unlike the big national supermarkets that lead the way on reflecting adopted cuisines and responding to trends, I had to get to the eighth page of Booths' recipes before I found a listed ingredient more exciting than cumin, smoked paprika or chorizo – and even then, it was only a fresh jalapeño in a Mexican-inspired cod dish. This is by no means an attack. After all, why should a place with so much good produce needlessly experiment with foods from other places? But on this meandering trip as I am, it just places Ilkley, as well as the bits of North Yorkshire I've been through, slightly at odds with what I've found almost everywhere else. My mind, of course, is already looking ahead to tomorrow, both to my trip to the butchery in Swaledale, and to the joyfully diverse cities of Bradford and Leeds barely ten miles away, in which I have long lists of restaurants to visit.

With Booths still on my mind, I find myself thinking about another British retail institution once I'm parked up in Leeds. It was in Leeds's Kirkgate Market that the Polish Jewish immigrant Michael Marks established his 'penny bazaar'; he would subsequently team up with a bookkeeper called Thomas Spencer to establish the Marks & Spencer we know and love. It may be a retail chain, but many of Marks's most iconic inventions loom large in British popular food culture, from Colin the Caterpillar and Percy Pig to some uniquely British culinary moments: a cheeky tin of G&T on the train, lunchtime meal deals for a day in the office. The kiosk in the market still 'operates' today, and as a man who has eaten more chicken kievs, yum yums and Percy Pigs than most would readily admit to, it is an honour to stand at the threshold of the monolith and pay my respects.

Unlike in other cities, the indoor market in Leeds has a vibrancy that is infectious. A tear still on my cheek from the penny bazaar, I career into a kiosk selling old-school Bakewell tarts and filled rolls, only just managing to avoid being mown down by a lad careening with a trolley laden with plantains, yams and Scotch bonnet chillies. I get a corned beef and red onion roll, partly to steady my nerves and partly to apologise for nearly knocking the till off its perch. It is pure joy mixed with an inexplicable nostalgia, for this is not a thing that I grew up on. And yet the fatty corned beef cut through with raw red onion has me reaching for a flat cap and tying my trousers with twine. And then in a heartbeat I turn another corner and am faced with a Jamaican patty spot with a queue up the whole aisle, then a Polish bakery piled high with rich breads, lots of glazed cakes and doughnuts, at least one of which is filled with apples and has my name written all over it. Round the next corner is Maxi's Rotisserie, a Chinese café renowned for its roasted meats, especially its char sui. And by the time I've completed a lap of the market I have a list that reads Karpaty, Fat Annie's, the Fisherman's Wife, Jenny's Jerk, Manjit's, Mr Mackerel, Banh & Mee and Khao Gaeng Thai. These are all places I need to try before leaving, which span Polish, Vietnamese, Thai, Jamaican, British, American, Indian and Turkish cuisine and reflect the cultural makeup of modern-day Leeds.

Towards the back of the market is a more modern street food area and it is here that I sit on a bench and make notes on everything I've just seen or eaten. I can confirm that the char sui pork at Maxi's is some of the most succulent I've ever tried. My intention was to have a mouthful or two and take the rest away with me, but the salty-sweet hit of the meat meant I just couldn't stop. I inhaled a beef patty from Jenny's Jerk, and I have a saltfish one in my coat pocket that will later have me beating the steering wheel of my car in exaltation. The thalis from Manjit's look gorgeous; a fella at a table across from me is head-down in pleasure eating one; when I ask, he tells me that they contain the only dhal other than his wife's that he eats – and not to tell her he does so. I get a banh mi and some summer rolls for later, too, but can't resist trying them as I make notes, the smoky pork in the sandwich a real joy against the sharp and spicy pickled carrots and chillies.

Despite pep talks to myself, I can't bring myself to eat anything else, but as I sit and observe the crowds queuing at the places I wish I could find the space to try, I conclude that almost anything bought from a place with a queue within this market will be great. If the people of Leeds return time and again, it must be. And the crowds here today are not tourists; these are people from here, and they offer votes of confidence with each queue they join, each dish they consume again and again. Surely one couldn't try what's on offer from all these places and leave without gout, self-loathing or IBS? Well, let me tell you, my self-esteem was in fine fettle as I strode out into the flat grey afternoon.

Leaving the market, I take a turn around the city centre to work off a little of my market excesses, and also to see what foods are popular here. I walk into a few establishments, safe in the knowledge that I will not be ordering a morsel to eat. Before long, I find myself trying to work out the common denominator for trendy spots. What makes them so different from the lively marketplaces like Kirkgate? In a lot of places I note menus that lean heavily towards brunches and offer a mix of typical British breakfast meats in rolls, butties, barms, buns or more esoteric breads such as flatbread or focaccia, combined in some way with an egg dish inspired by Mexican or Middle Eastern flavours. The inclusion of chipotle, za'atar, jalapeño or hummus seems to justify inflated prices.

I've noted this previously, but it fascinates me more here, because what actually makes a place trendy? I suppose it's a self-consciousness – the menu is meant to reflect an identity based on what the owners consider cool, which in turn reflects how we like to see ourselves. Just as a social-media foodie performatively curates what they eat for their audience, the menu choices are deliberate here, and very different from those in the old-school market. Kirkgate doesn't put on airs; its traders know who they are, and they're not jumping on trends. Compared to the market, the dishes on offer on the high street don't reflect much except the naturalisation of core ingredients from storied and complex cuisines into bastardised versions of things that were once great. What is British food now? It is a handful of 'Mexican' flavours – coriander, chipotle and lime – thrown carelessly at eggs or pork and called Brunch. It is the whole of North Africa, Turkey, Greece and the Middle East, thrown together in a lightly spiced medley of halloumi, hummus, pickles and spices and variously described in chaotic ways for your lunch. And it is the narrowest slither of the kimchi, gochujang and fried chicken end of Korean food, approximated into dishes we already recognise but are now willing to have with slightly more spice for dinner.

I'm probably being unfair. Any integration of a new cuisine or ingredient into a national cuisine will take decades – from excited adoption, through awkward adaptation, to complete assimilation. And it is not a linear process. Early adopters vigorously promote it, defend it to the death and then deride it once it reaches mass popularity. The second wave of adopters will inevitably end up doing bizarre things with the food once they've decided it's a good thing, adding gochujang to lasagnas or 'nduja to bowls of ramen, and this is where early adopters decry inauthenticity, appropriation or over-exposure. Before long, the mass market adopters have become bored and have moved on to a new thing, at which point the early adopters can reclaim the trend and return it to its rightful home. Or the thing might now have a new life of its own. In this case, both early adopters and adapters decide the thing is too good to let go of; the white-hot heat of its introduction might ease off, but it will be on supermarket shelves, in ready meals, in restaurants and as new dishes that bear little resemblance to the original thing. Before you realise, the trend has properly entered British cuisine, a position it will hold for decades. Not many things make it this far, which is why changing a nation's cuisine is a glacial process. Mexican, Middle Eastern and Korean food are in that awkward middle phase of their adoption life cycle. Only time will tell which dishes will hold – which will go the way of Peruvian food and slip from popular consciousness, and which will stick and take on a life of their own, as ramen has? And it is a reminder for me to give these things a break, to ease off on my frustration when things are clumsily handled or crowbarred awkwardly on to menus. These are foods in flux and need to be allowed to find their final form.

Before I leave Leeds, I must pop into the Turk's Head (or Whitelock's, depending on who told you about it), the oldest pub in the city and a place John Betjeman called 'the very heart of Leeds'. It sits down an alleyway opposite JD Sports and between two phone shops, and as I sip my half of Kirkstall Pale I can't help but feel deflated by the juxtaposition of Kirkgate Market and the chains, brunch spots and concept restaurants I see as I walk about. Despite my jubilation at the breadth, energy and authenticity of the market, there remains a feeling of latent resistance to its continued success. That just beyond the market, where so many are engaged in the earnest production of something good that reflects their culinary heritage, most customers are spending their money in investor-backed concepts where the food comes from a central kitchen and is reheated before being sold at an extortionate price is at best frustrating, at worst devastating.

Here in Leeds, the demographic growth is coming from Brits with Pakistani, Indian and Bangladeshi heritage, but also from Polish, Slovak, Czech and Yemeni communities. Add to that migration from Jamaica, Iraq, Kurdistan, Syria and Somalia and we have a group of cultures with rich culinary heritage, all of which can be sampled along the Leeds Road connecting the city to Bradford.

As I crawl along in my car, the traffic giving me a chance to take in restaurants lining the road, what is most noticeable, and most exciting to me, are the businesses that I see with very similar names and stylings to more well-known businesses around the country. In among the betting shops and fried chicken spots that are ubiquitous on almost all British high streets, here you'll find businesses such as Mahmood's, a burger chain known for its Big Dripper and with stylings that recall a fast-food chain known for its golden arches. Up the road is Frangoz, its name bringing to mind Nando's, its menu reflecting something more complex – it shares stylings with Popeyes, KFC and indeed, Nando's, but with a unique take that makes it very much its own thing. Two highlights stood out from my visit to Frangoz: first, the Blue Taki Taki Burger, a fried chicken creation that uses hot cheese sauce and fiery Blue Heat Takis to create a burger that is so overwhelmingly crunchy, spicy and MSG-laden that it's hard to think straight while you're eating it. It's a fever dream, a literal torching of your taste buds that leaves you wanting it to stop while also wanting more. Second, in a move that no one would advise, I also ordered two of

Frangoz's bestselling pizzas, which stood out as being both uniquely British and very much reflective of their creators' heritage: a Desi Spice pizza topped with tandoori chicken, spiced beef, peppers and cheese, and a Donner pizza that is exactly what it sounds like, fine strands of perfectly rendered, processed lamb on a solid version of a takeaway pizza – what's not to love?

It'd be easy to sneer at this menu – after all, at its core, it's little more than amped-up fast food taken to its radical extremes. However, social media is full of content that depicts street vendors running wild with invented dishes that take a carb and combine it with an apparently random snack from their local corner store. From the beloved Mexican tradition of Tostilocos, a street food in which a bag of nacho-flavoured Tostitos are cut open and topped with cucumber, pickled or crispy pork skin, lime juice, hot sauce, chamoy, Tajín chilli powder, salt and Japanese peanuts, to the creativity of Hawaii's snacks made with Spam, there's some genius in the back of a corner shop everywhere from India, Thailand and Vietnam, to Korea, Malaysia and Indonesia, creating delicious madness by combining recently arrived treats with traditional foodstuffs. Nowadays, it is globalisation and an increase in long-haul travel rather than sending your soldiers to another country that help a Japanese snack arrive in Wakefield or a British confectionery make it to a street vendor in Manila. And when these things do wash up on our shores, nothing is more British than immediately adapting them to our tastes. Which is how Takis, the spicy rolled-tortilla crisps that have made a splash in the UK over the last couple of years, as well as kebabs, desi spices and other non-Italian flavours, should wind up as pizza toppings, such is our love for the medium. Of course, this is nothing new. In places with thriving diaspora communities, things like Masala pizzas or Pide pizzas have been part of our high streets for as long as I've been alive. But how joyful to see it carried off in Frangoz with such panache, and for it to feel not like a novelty but a seamless reflection of a place and how a local palate has developed.

My final stop along the Leeds Road is Leeds Road Fisheries, a firm favourite in these parts for the past twenty-five years, and a business at the heart of the community. I am here for its menu though, which is like Frangoz but in an even more authentic and organic sense, a marvel of improving on a thing that is already popular. This is ostensibly a fish and chip shop, and though you can still get a classic cod and chips if that's what you want, it is also a pizza spot, kebab shop, fried chicken spot and more. If a list of pizzas that includes Special Fish (masala fish on a pizza), Keema, Keema & Achar, Chicken Boti, Donner, Seafood and Caribbean doesn't excite and intrigue you, I don't know what would.

The thing that catches my eye on the big yellow sign above the door is Masala Fish – and that's what I'm here for. My friend George, an extraordinary chef and once a schoolboy in Bradford, tells me that it is one of the finest bites of food in Yorkshire. I order it and am offered a choice of chips, pitta or naan. I opt for naan in a panic, and am not disappointed as I watch a naan the size of my torso get softened on a grill while my masala fish is fried (or grilled, I can't quite tell). Eating it in the car, it has a beautifully balanced spicing, and a delicate bark that could be a result of either deep frying or a hard grilling on a flat top.

I'm cross with myself for not asking more about the spicing and how the fish is cooked, so I decide to go back and ask. When I finally get to the front of the queue for a second time, I tell them I'm writing a book about British food and they tell me to mind my own business. It's a secret recipe, and they're busy. So I retreat. Fair enough, I think. They don't need my help – they are full from noon to night, and why should they give away their cherished secrets? You'll just have to try it for yourselves.

Having greedily chomped through a decent portion of masala fish, I think I've worked out that the fish has been marinated in a blend of chilli, garam masala, garlic and ginger, before being dipped in a spiced batter and fried to golden perfection. Simple. And British? Well, if fried fish descended from Sephardic Jewish recipes that were brought to East London from Spain and Portugal in the 1800s is British, then fish in chilli and garam masala surely is too.

*

Now I need to get to Skipton before the butchers clock off for the day at Swaledale; I'm keen to discover exactly what the team who source and butcher some of the finest meat in the country eat for their breakfast, lunch and dinner.

Apart from fish and chips, is there anything more British than butchery? The Sunday roast is, for many, the cornerstone of the Great British Week. Roast beef and Yorkshire pudding, Cumberland sausages for toad in the hole, black pudding, lamb and mint sauce, bacon. The Worshipful Company of Butchers was formed in 975 AD – a very long time ago, for those keeping score – so butchery has been a central pillar of British society for a bloody long time. And it remains a tradition that we hold dear, even as we allow supermarkets and the downward pressures of capitalism to destroy it.

Swaledale, for all its commitment to supporting small-scale farmers, promoting heritage and native livestock breeds, and practising and promoting whole-carcass, nose-to-tail butchery, is based in a light industrial unit a mile or so outside Skipton. This is not the world of ornately tiled butchers' shops, sides of meat hanging from hooks in the window. This is butchery as it was meant to be, practised close to where the animals are reared and then killed, and carried out with small-scale farmers so that the butcher knows the animal, the farmer and the customer.

I hug my friend George in the car park of the

industrial complex just as a fresh batch of carcasses arrives from the nearby abattoir. It's good timing for a delivery, and I ask George if we can follow the meat on a blow-by-blow tour through Swaledale's process. I quickly feel like a side of beef myself, for we literally grab one and haul it on to a chain-operated pulley system, before pushing it along the journey that all beef follows at Swaledale. After an initial butchering, it goes into storage, out again to be broken down into prime cuts and other bits, then back into a fridge for ageing or into a room for packing and labelling; finally it will end up back in a van destined for one of the UK's best restaurants, or in a small brown box that will be sent via post to a lucky sod who'll cook it at home. And as we pass in and out of these rooms, we are met by butchers wearing chainmail and wielding technically shaped knives. I find myself losing sensitivity for what the product is, and instead focus on the skill and care and passion of the butchers, but also the monotony of the process, their knowledgeable detachment. These guys are not hipsters with Instagram feeds full of photos of bucolic farm visits. This is skilled butchery as a job, a profession not unlike being a mechanic, a teacher or a personal trainer. And there's something both enticing and grounding in that.

My tour through the abattoir over, we retreat to the office upstairs to discuss the stats behind who buys Swaledale's meat – and what that tells us about British tastes. In the middle of the table is a massive box of tremendous-looking savoury pastries from the butcher's in town. They get them in once or twice a week, I understand, as a little lunch treat for the team. I'm offered one and reach for a hefty-looking 'slice' that I expect is likely to contain steak.

'What you gone for?' the office manager asks from across the office.

'No idea. Steak slice, I guess.'

'Hope not, for your sake,' she says.

'What should I have gone for?'

'None of 'em are great, truth be told.'

I take a bite of a steak slice that is, as she suggested, not the best.

'See,' she says. 'Not great, is it?'

'Which are most popular?' I ask, sensing that I'm on the cusp of some genuine social anthropological research.

'The steak pie is the one they all go for.'

'OK, maybe I'll try that.'

'That's the one you've already tried. They all have quite bland tastes.'

'So, what's your favourite?' I ask, feeling deflated, but hopeful of snatching something useful from this exchange.

'Probably the steak pie, to be fair. I make my own lunch though, mainly.'

'Don't even ask,' George says, sensing my desperation. 'Honestly, some of the dietary choices of the team here will melt your brain.'

'Can I ask them?' I venture. 'That's exactly what I want to know. What do people actually eat? Not when they're chefs, or foodies. What do people eat who just have to eat?'

'You've come to the right place for that,' the office manager says. 'I eat a cheese roll most days, or a cheese salad.'

My instinct is to ask for details. What cheese? What salad leaves? Anything else in the roll? She pre-empts my enthusiasm though, pricking it with one deft swipe.

'I love cheese. Just Cheddar, mind. The Cathedral one, the red one, or the little mini ones if I can't be arsed.'

A second later, one of the butchers from downstairs has his head round the door.

'Tell 'im about lunch. What you eat,' the office manager says, nodding in my direction.

'Pie,' he says, as if I'm asking a very stupid question.

'What about at home? After work? What's on the table?' I try.

'Depends on day of t'week.'

'Tonight?'

'Wednesday, in't? Roast.'

'Not on a Sunday?'

'Both. Grandad likes a roast on Wednesday.'

'What about other nights?'

'Mum does a pie some nights, or sausages. If she's working I get pizza.'

A minute or so later, a new face. 'Right, who wants to know about cooking?'

'I'm researching a book,' I say to the ruddy chap peering around the door. 'Like, do you cook? What would you make for yourself after work?'

'I cook every night,' the new face says. 'Love it.'

'Amazing. What sort of thing?'

'Anything really. Spag bol, stir-fries. Not rice, I hate rice. But noodles, veggies, bit of sauce. Or pasta. Loads of pasta. Healthy stuff, you know.'

'How do you know how to cook?'

'YouTube.'

'You do all the cooking?'

'Missus hates cooking. I love it.'

And with that, the face is gone.

I ended up speaking to almost all the butchers and the wider team at Swaledale, and apart from George, who is a fully trained chef and someone who cares about meat, where it comes from and how to cook it, no one seemed to care much about what they ate, least of all had anything but a passing interest in what people anywhere else in the country ate or about whether what they ate said anything about them and where they live. And why would they?

It was a sobering and humbling experience. Some of them might have been playing to the crowd a little, but most were just busy people who didn't mince their words. And apart from making me feel a little bit silly for caring so much about what we eat, it made me think about how we came to lose the connection with our own food history. Would a visit to a large Italian butchery business have played out the same way? I doubt it. Nor in France, Spain, Italy, Greece, Portugal, and the rest.

This is not a slur on the people I spoke to. We have such a disconnect in our food system in this country that it might have felt weirder if they'd had a deep passion for the specifics of beef cookery, or lists of unusual ways with pork mince. Of course a young man living on his own in Skipton will eat pizza most nights unless his mum is cooking a roast dinner or a pie. Of course a cheese roll or a bought-in steak pie is what most people eat for lunch, because what is the alternative? Skipton, from what I could see, has a Morrisons Local, a Greggs, a handful of coffee shops and a Tesco superstore on the edge of town. There are a few Indian and Chinese takeaways, a load of takeaway pizza places, and some nicely dressed restaurants up the high street, along with a couple of coffee shops and something akin to a deli. I know that there's a thriving community of allotment holders in Skipton. But if you're a young person learning to cook for yourself in a food landscape that's a series of takeaways, chains and the 'express' style of supermarket where the small veg section is all plastic-wrapped and Pot Noodles and ready meals are much cheaper, well, you're pretty fucked, aren't you? And in interviewing these young butchers, that's one picture that emerges. It's not their fault that the food system is broken – but it's a sad corner of what British food is.

Before leaving this chapter behind, it is important to note the extraordinary work that Swaledale and all the butchers like them do, up and down the country. As a country, we have become divorced from the farmers and the butchers who are responsible for the meat we consume – and no one but the supermarkets is to blame. Since the 1970s, when they began selling meat after the post-rationing meat boom of the 1960s, the percentage of low-quality meat we eat has risen in direct correlation to the decline in high-street butchers. And where a butcher will buy whole animals and make use of as much of the animal as they can, a supermarket is in the business of ensuring that the most popular cuts of meat are available to everyone, from the first customer through the door in the morning to the last customer at night. It's no wonder that variety is not an option, and this has meant that we've lost the taste for a broad range of things – and the skill of cooking them. And in order to satisfy the huge demand for chicken breasts, we have to develop a system that can deliver as many properly sized chicken breasts as quickly and cheaply as possible. As a result, we've lost the connection between farmers and customers, the knowledgeable butcher, and thus the connection between what we eat and the land. Thank god, then, for Swaledale and its farmers, for butchers and the farmers that serve them.

While I was in the cold room with George, staring at

racks of meat, he did reveal to me that British consumer habits have changed. Lamb has become prohibitively expensive. Beef is a back-to-front game: all the trendy offcuts such as skirt, onglet and short ribs are now expensive, some of the old-school cuts less so. Pork sells, but mainly as sausage or bacon. And chicken outsells everything else, but we prefer it broken down now more than whole – a fact that is true for meats across the board. And so with that, my time in Yorkshire is up. Time to head south.

4

The North-West

Manchester is a prime example of how we don't properly appreciate what's good in the UK. If they spoke a foreign language up here, people would talk excitedly about how we really must come for a long weekend. We'd be feverishly booking flights the minute Ryanair posted its newest deals. There'd be lists of the five best coffee shops, the ten dishes in Manchester you must try before you die, the twenty-five reasons you should quit your job, pack the car and head north to live the famous Manc lifestyle.

For all of that, Manchester is probably the city after London whose food culture has been most shaped by gentrification, rising rents and hype. It's a glorious foodie destination, but not everyone in Manchester can eat like this every day. I've seen more homelessness in the city centre than anywhere else in the country; as I walk along the river in Ancoats in a gentrified bubble, I know this isn't the full picture – but where is? Talk to diners, restaurateurs and the upwardly mobile here and you'll find a city that has never been so full of energy, verve and direction.

All You Can Eat

*

Before all that, a word on Crewe, the portrait in the attic to Manchester's Dorian Gray. Approaching Manchester from the south, it seems silly to ignore the opportunities presented by the juxtaposition of the big city above and the little, once busy town below – especially given my aim to explore the full spectrum of our food culture.

Crewe has long been one of the major rail hubs in Britain. The station was built in 1937; it has twelve platforms, and everything in Crewe owes its existence to the trains. It might not be a main city station, but Crewe is a key connection point where lines diverge to Manchester Piccadilly and off into North Wales, and it's the last major station before the Liverpool branch. The modern town was built to service the railway, and Crewe is still the home of the original Rolls Royce factory; cars built right next to the station could be sent all over the country. Nowadays, the factory largely produces Bentleys, a fact that seems more bizarre the longer you spend in Crewe. I didn't see many Bentleys in the street.

Crewe's major interchange energy has my mood lifting; as I head into town, I'm struck again by how large its station is compared to the relatively small town it serves. It reminds me of Clapham Junction: no one loves the area around it, but I know from experience that there's some very fine food within walking distance if you know where to go. Could Crewe have the same hidden depths? Might a sleeper foodie destination be available for those who can walk a little from the station?

The first road I walk down doesn't promise much, but I forge on, thinking of Clapham. And in fact, Crewe has a good-sized Polish and Eastern European community, if the number of shops and little supermarkets on the way into town are anything to go by. In fact, when I stopped in for a drink these were by far the most welcoming businesses of anywhere I visited here. I'm only in Crewe for a short time, and so I'm not in the mindset of buying bits and pieces to cook for an evening meal, but I was pleased to find the freezer sections of these shops filled with yeast dumplings, carp and chicken hearts alongside a more typical selection of frozen chips, peas, garlic bread and ice lollies. If I ever find myself trapped in Crewe with no means of immediate escape, I would ransack one or two of these stores and live for a while on chicken hearts, skewered and grilled and served with sauerkraut and mustard, or ajvar and parsley salad. I might make pike balls in mustard sauce, and I'd certainly slow-cook a pork knuckle and steam some yeast dumplings in the liquor. I'd be happy for a good while cooking good Eastern European staples, and clearly the people of Crewe are doing this too.

I pass up on adding a bag of frozen yeast dumplings to my backpack, but can't resist a multipack of Polish Princo Polo chocolate bars. With my blood sugar spiking, I continue my voyage of discovery.

As I'm walking I make a note of the nearly one hundred restaurants of every cuisine and persuasion I pass along the way. It being the daytime, very few are open, so I cannot pass judgement on how good they are, but I am struck that the selection reflects what British cuisine is becoming; here, on the grey streets of Crewe, we have every iteration of every food trend that can be seen in every major city and on every form of social media. This is the restaurant selection you might end up with if you locked Andrew Tate and Steven Bartlett in a boardroom and tasked them with designing their perfect culinary high street; we have a high street full of concepts based on corporate profit as opposed to taste, pleasure or for the good of customers.

Piri piri, smash burgers, new-wave pizza concepts, American BBQ that is anything but, Korean, Vietnamese and Thai street food concepts, and the same again from India, Sri Lanka and Malaysia. And there are the fusions, confusions of myriad cuisines reductively labelled only as Asian this or Asian that. And all of it leans hard on neon, gaudy vinyls and backlit menu boards, with very few places making much noise about their cooks, their produce or promoting themselves as showcasing the best of a cuisine. No doubt most of these poor buggers have been duped into a franchise model dreamed up in Canary Wharf and tested in a Westfield somewhere, but I'm here to tell you the footfall numbers aren't translating to midweek Crewe. Of course, many of these fast-food places will rely on scootering or e-biking their wares to every corner of Crewe – closer to dark kitchens, those faceless hubs that only exist to allow the efficient production of popular dishes, than restaurants. Still, judging by the peeling vinyl and dust-laden counters of many of these restaurants, I'd say the hope of taking Crewe by storm died within a year of the ink drying on the franchise agreement.

Alongside the takeaways with garish branding, Crewe has its share of the usual British comforts: greasy spoon, kebab shop, Chinese takeaway and Indian restaurant. As anywhere in the UK, these kinds of places tend to telegraph their Britishness on the signs above the door, but we know the greasy spoon is likely run by Greeks, Poles, Albanians or Turks. The kebab shop is the same. The Chinese restaurant might be Cantonese at heart but with dishes added from elsewhere over time, and the Indian restaurant is likely Bangladeshi and thriving.

And so as I make it back to the car to continue north, my plan to stop in Wilmslow on my way to Manchester, I am again left to reflect on what my sojourn in Crewe has taught me. Again, almost all signs of 'British' food as my grandparents might have recognised it have gone. The pubs on my route offered crisps and foreign lager, mainly; the shops and corner stores reflected the tastes and the home-cooking of new communities, but aside from the lottery and the fags behind the counter they had little in common with a Britain even of the early

2000s. I couldn't see any old-fashioned butchers, bakers or greengrocers; for the first time anywhere, I saw not a single coffee shop, which meant no new-wave baked goods that might have carried the torch for local food. Perhaps only the caffs still offer up something of a typical British nostalgia. And so what instead? Well, for the people of Crewe, it seems, we have identikit takeaway franchises all offering things we've seen elsewhere, heavily handicapped by supply chains, earnings models and trend data. These don't reflect the demands of the people on the streets. Like battery hens though, we sip at the teat we are proffered – and slowly, the spreadsheets win. The spreadsheets can afford rents that are slightly higher than they should be, so people from here get priced out, and thus the little spots that might organically emerge don't appear, and the old family-run places shut their doors. Instead, a hungry visitor will meet seven empty Piri Piri chicken franchises and four smash burger spots in a two-hundred-yard stretch of high street. Without an opportunity to get something better, as I leave Crewe I find myself with a W H Smith's meal deal to eat in the car. There was literally no other workable option for a good lunch – or at least not without having a microwave or steamer to fashion some of those delicious frozen yeast dumplings on the back seat.

Say what you like about hipsters and the gentrifying masses, but they play a role in ensuring a version of decent food is available on almost any high street, in any city. I'd take that over the franchise factory I found in Crewe.

And so to Wilmslow. The eastern point on a golden triangle that houses the most expensive houses in the north-west is home to an Aston Martin showroom that outsells any other stockist in the country. I have no idea what to expect, but I know that Peter Crouch and Abbey Clancy once lived here, and so I have notions of it being leafy and glamorous. It is, and the high street is littered with high-end boutiques, nail bars and hair salons. I'm here to try the town's food, of course, but I can't help but hope to see Gary Neville picking up his dry cleaning or Jesse Lingard parking his sports car outside the Caribbean restaurant he owns on the high street.

Within two minutes of parking I'm nearly run over by a large black 4 × 4, which isn't the welcome I was hoping to receive. The centre of Wilmslow is marked out by a few underwhelming landmarks that give the place a workable boundary. Its easternmost point is marked by the station and a leisure centre, the westernmost by the Aston Martin dealership. To the north there is a Waitrose, to the south a Sainsbury's. Between all of that is a high street that holds all the trappings of every salubrious suburban high street up and down the country. Wellness and beauty treatments are prevalent, as are boutiques and restaurants. But I'm here for the restaurants. If the lack of decent fare in Crewe speaks to the way that socio-economic factors have shaped modern British food, the restaurants in Wilmslow tell us something else about how money shapes taste in the UK. I've noticed this elsewhere, but it's most obvious here, having been to places at either end of the spectrum in a single day. Crewe and Wilmslow are only about an hour from each other, but they're worlds apart culinarily as well as economically. The food offering in a place like Crewe, be it in shops or restaurants, reflects the people who live there. When the population changes, it quickly leads to shifts in local cuisine. I made light of the franchised horror show that I found there, but despite all of that, the shops and the few independent food businesses were aimed at, owned and operated by the people who live there. In Wilmslow and most other places like it, the restaurants don't reflect the home-cooking of the people who live there, but instead the places they've been to on holiday or travel to for work. Big restaurants that could be in Milan, Santorini or a Parisian back street, little spots that serve ramen, Caribbean food, tacos or big North African or Middle Eastern salads. The style of places is not homely and humble; it is big and brash and shiny. Some of the places might be concepts, they might be destined to be franchised (for that seems to be the ultimate aim of all food businesses nowadays), but they are all open, slick and full of customers who, even on their work lunch breaks, have the tanned and scented air of holiday, the far away ease of the corporate traveller. Wilmslow is a wealthy place, which of course helps. I am not here to assess whether it is right or not that Crewe had the gait of a person one disappointment away from collapse, while Wilmslow has the assurance of a person with a tax adviser and an investment portfolio. But it is a fact that a Greek restaurant or a ramen spot in Wilmslow does not reflect a thriving Greek or Japanese diaspora, while the Polish shops or Vietnamese nail bars in Crewe are reflective of buoyant local diaspora communities. And for my money, this follows through into the food cooked locally, and thus what might be called British food here. Communities living, shopping and eating in a place will always have more of an impact on the food offered than a restaurant cherry-picking its menu from a wholesale supply chain.

So Wilmslow is charming, but it doesn't have the grit in the oyster that in other places would make it a pearl. For my part I stop at Jerk Junction, keen to try something to snap me out of the funk Crewe has placed me in. I discover later that this is the place owned by the aforementioned Jesse Lingard, one-time Manchester United footballer now plying his trade in South Korea, and Miss Ivy, a Jamaican chef who has made Manchester and the surrounding area worship at the altar of her creations since she moved here twenty-five years ago. I order a very good goat curry, and am uplifted. I am not quite transported to a painted bench with my feet being lapped by a temperate sea; I am still in Wilmslow, in sight of a Gail's Bakery and serviced offices to rent, but I am restored. The goat curry is fragrant with pimento and thyme, lifted by curry powder, and has all the heat you'd expect from a Scotch bonnet chilli, leaving me full and with the chapstick smile of any fatty, slow-cooked meat dish.

It reminds me how under-appreciated Caribbean food is within our country. A sentence that might upset some, I know, but it's true – too few of us give Caribbean food its due. Consider how widely the foods of almost every community which has moved to this country have taken hold. Even the most disinterested diner will have tried at some point dishes of Indian origin, Chinese, Vietnamese, Thai, Italian, Greek, Portuguese, and so on. And yet despite this, for so many of us Caribbean cuisine has not crossed over into the British diet. There has been immigration to the UK from the Caribbean for as long as we've been exploiting their islands for resources; sailors, slaves and labourers arrived in the UK from the eighteenth century, not to mention the tens of thousands who fought for Britain in both world wars and beyond. It's a long relationship, and so for us to have kept such an extraordinary and delicious cuisine at arm's length for this long points to something fishy in our psyche.

I can't speak for anyone else, but all I know is that considering the scale of immigration to this country from the Caribbean, and given the number of Brits with roots there, it is odd that we don't have more of the Caribbean's extraordinary cuisine in the canon of British delights. I've never seen its dishes in a listicle of quintessential British dishes.

The North-West

This train of thought was triggered when I walked back to the car and noticed a crowd of people outside a single establishment, something I've noticed time and again on high streets during this trip. In among the high-end sushi of Zumuku, the glitzy Thai of Naa Kin, the chi-chi Greek vision of the Stolen Lamb and the starched collars and white jeans at the Italian-leaning Cibo Gran Café, here, in Wilmslow – as in nearly three hundred other locations across Britain – sits another vision for the future of our national cuisine.

On first passing it, I did not enter. I did, though, record a voice note in my phone that simply said: 'Who or what is Lounges, and what does it say about British food today?'

The answer (having spent hours looking at their menus, their stated aims and their success as laid out in Companies House filings) is that they are the new Wetherspoons – not that Wetherspoons itself is going anywhere.

Operating from morning to night, and catering to the casual British diner's every whim, they have popped up in 281 locations up and down the country – and the brand is worth hundreds of million pounds as a result. Unlike Wetherspoons, the modus operandi of Lounges is not serving short-sell-by-date beer at suspiciously low prices. Unlike Wetherspoons, a Lounges is not dowdy nor devoid of music or entertainment. Lounges is a mood board of animal print wallpaper, in a setting that embraces noise, clatter and chaos; what it has in common with Wetherspoons is that they are both engaged in the stack-'em-high-sell-'em-low model of appealing to the masses, meeting customers where they are.

For someone looking to analyse what British food is, the menu of a place like Lounges reveals a great deal about how the benchmark of what's considered normal has shifted since the millennium. Lounges is not a place with an affiliation towards any particular cuisine. Like Wetherspoons in the late 1990s and early 2000s, it is a reflection of our tastes, aimed at being somewhere that's comforting and where we know we're getting something familiar. If the Wetherspoons offering of my teenage years saw fry-ups, curry nights and beer-and-burger deals as the staples that reflected our tastes, the Lounges menu of today shows just where our magpie preferences have taken us.

Breakfast at Lounges offers: four versions of a fry-up, shakshuka, a quesadilla, a pancake stack, smashed avocado on toast and something called a Miami brunch that I guess is Cuban-influenced given the South American leanings of the ingredients. So British, Middle Eastern, Mediterranean, Mexican, American and Australian influences at breakfast. For the rest of the day, the menu is designed to please as many people as possible. In today's Britain that means burgers – a section that plays out largely as you would expect, although the addition of a Korean burger and the presence of chorizo, jalapeños, chipotle mayo and halloumi are of interest. A selection of sandwiches consists of two

The North-West

panini, a ciabatta and a burrito. Then there is tapas, which despite being mostly Spanish includes two Korean-inspired choices and a kofte plate that would normally belong on a mezze. There's a choice of five salads, including a mezze bowl, a buddha bowl and a chicken, bacon and avocado salad. Finally, there's a list of mains that includes an orzo-based dish, buttermilk fried chicken, nasi goreng, slow-cooked brisket chilli con carne, steak frites and a Korean-inspired fried chicken dish.

So is this the optimised menu for the modern British palate? As the UK's fastest-growing casual restaurant chain, anyone interested in the future of food in this country should be paying attention to what Lounges tells us about the new normal. Like Wetherspoons before it, Lounges is not focused on attracting tourists. It's not for special occasions – it's pitched as a home away from home. Between the desertification of Crewe and the jet set tastes of Wilmslow, Lounges is somewhere in the middle, catering to – well, everyone. Lounges restaurants don't exist in urban areas where a bulk of diners are only there for a meal, a weekend at the most, and therefore play into ease, noisy promotions and gimmicks to snare passing trade. No, Lounges are on suburban high streets, they exist for the people in those places, they exist to be a comfort, a treat perhaps, but mainly to be the place you can go with your friends, your family, and where everyone can have something they enjoy.

And the noticeable absences from the Lounges menu? Indian flavours, Chinese influences, Thai dishes – once the staple of the first generation of gastropubs. Aside from the fry-ups, there's hardly anything that might have once been described as British. In their place? Plenty of Italian influence, a lasting infatuation with American flavours – made sexy by borrowing willy-nilly from Mexico – plenty of nods to Greek, Turkish and Middle Eastern dishes, and a huge shift towards the naughty-fireworks-and-chilli-heat of Korean food.

So that's what the data-led consultants think British food is nowadays, and in some ways it's hard to disagree.

Before I leave Wilmslow and head to Manchester, I must reference the other middle-class joy factory that exists on nearly as many British high streets as Lounges and Wetherspoons: Cook. It's a business I last noticed as a child, when a shiny new store opened near where I grew up in Tunbridge Wells. Back then, I dismissed Cook as a posh Iceland, but now I must re-evaluate – at least to assess what it says about British food. Its survival on high streets is enough to tell me it has got something very right. And so, as I stand in the aisle of the Wilmslow branch, wedged between two chest freezers wrapped in images of bucolic propaganda, of British scenes replete with farmyards, grazing lambs and dry-stone walls, I flick through their catalogue and marvel at another data-led exercise in catering for the masses.

Here the scene is the same, but different. In the

kitchens of middle-class homes, it seems, the tethers to the past are stronger than in other places I have visited on this journey. At the front of the brochure are pages offering a 20 per cent discount on bestsellers, a slightly claustrophobic list that brings to mind sticky leather Volvos, warm elderflower cordial, singed oven gloves and damp labradors stinking up a house from in front of a cream Aga range: cottage pie, chicken and leek pie, lasagna, beef bourguignon, chicken tikka masala and fish pie. So far, so 90s-home-county-supper. Flicking a few pages on, though, one can find dhal, Thai curries, a teriyaki rice and a sweet potato katsu that would struggle to entice even the most ardent Wagamama fan.

On turning to a page that promises 'NEW! Pan Asian Meals delivered', I stand, open-mouthed. I pop the catalogue into my bag and retreat to the car to make my way to Manchester, where I will study this piece of extraordinary social history in more detail.

My first stop in the city is Pollen Bakery, a place I've been excited to visit since following them on Instagram as I began the research for this book. Launched in 2016, Pollen started, as game-changing things often do, in a railway arch under Manchester Piccadilly station. Founded by two home-baking obsessives, it produces the best sourdough loaf I've ever had the pleasure of chewing through. The Pollen sourdough has a crackle-glazed crust, brittle and shiny to look at, darkly roasted and chewy. Originally, they only sold this extraordinary bread and some equally mind-altering pastries. They now have two sites, one in Ancoats, the other in a development called Kampus, which is where I'm sitting. All exposed concrete and lights strung across the ceiling on long wires, Pollen feels more like the places you seek out on long weekends in Berlin or Copenhagen than a bakery in Manchester. I order a coffee, a pain au chocolat, a loaf of their twenty-eight-hour sourdough, a hockey puck of a cookie and a gold-gilded cookie dough brownie, finding a seat in the corner where I can be left alone to spike my blood sugar and work through the Cook brochure that has so captured my fascination.

The Pan Asian meals according to Cook include laab, katsu, laksa, rendang, ramen, mapo tofu and teriyaki. Buzzwords generated through data-mining the nation's search histories? Sure. Questionable execution of these dishes? Likely. An indication of the direction of British tastes? Certainly.

Having expected to be hard-wired to the Cook brochure for the foreseeable, I noted only two more things in the pamphlet before returning to my coffee and pastries. One, Cook – and by association the middle classes of the UK – still love a bit of good British game, represented here by twelve duck and two venison dishes (en croute and casserole, since you ask) that reflect the British game season as it develops. And two, the chapter titles of the booklet read as follows: Cuisines – Indian meals, Thai meals, Pies, Italian Meals, Classic British Meals, Pan Asian Meals and Game. Before I

The North-West

leave Pollen, sugared and jittery but sated, I Google the offering at Charlie Bigham's, the only other mass-market middle-class offering that rivals Cook. In fact, in the Home Counties, I imagine you can count on one hand the number of homes that haven't had a Cook or Charlie Bigham's ready meal in the last year. In addition to the list of cuisines that Cook deem tempting to the British palate, the only addition at Bingham's is Spanish – and he doesn't seem to go in for the Asian cuisines that Cook have introduced, with a single Thai dish and nothing else from that continent. What strikes me most about these bellwethers of mid-market British consumption is that there is no reflection of Caribbean food, nothing from the Middle East, and nothing from Eastern Europe. I say this without judgement, but it does reinforce my earlier thoughts on Caribbean food. It's curious, isn't it, how we decide what we will and won't adopt.

Up and out of Pollen bakery, I have a list as long as your inside leg of neighbourhoods, restaurants, places and shops I want to visit. I start to head west towards Medlock Canteen, a trendy spot (sadly now closed but heaving when I visited – a fact that reflects how tough it is to run a restaurant in the UK nowadays, even a busy and hyped one). Medlock offered enticing treats all day long. It might have been called a diner if this was America, but here we can safely call Medlock an all-day restaurant, a place that serves exactly the food you crave at exactly the right moment of the day, be that a burger at breakfast time or a bacon sandwich, hash browns and a milkshake for dinner. It was a good spot to consider what British food is, and it's a spot that tells you that – for the creators and customers of Medlock, at least – it is proper breakfasts of pork pies and sausage rolls, eggs and various carbs and accompaniments that are largely English rather than Scandi or Australian. There was nothing cinnamon-scented nor avocado-adjacent, though a French influence was in evidence – if the few-hundred-year-association between Brits and hollandaise over eggs can still be considered French. For lunch and beyond, the menu was British in terms of ingredients, but with a low level of East and West Coast American influence in attitude and menu language.

I didn't manage to eat at Medlock Canteen on this trip, because Manchester's Chinatown got its hooks into me. By the time I'd hauled myself out of the last Asian supermarket, I had to prioritise making it to a few more parts of the city before I beat my retreat. Did I learn much in Manchester's Chinatown about what British food is now? I did not. It is a thriving part of the city; Manchester's Chinese communities are long established and their institutions much loved. Alongside the traditional Cantonese style of Chinese restaurant, there exists a second wave of regional speciality spots. Added to these are Malaysian and Malaysian-Chinese spots, Korean places, plenty of good Japanese restaurants, and more, showing a city that is alive with new influence and demand for the good stuff. Long-time residents might bemoan the changing face of Manchester's Chinatown and the loss of its purely Chinese identity, but it has not been Disneyfied – it has just moved with the times.

From this south-western part of the city I headed north, aimed at Climat, a highly regarded restaurant, and the National Football Museum, one of the country's best museums – at least for a lifelong member of the Surrey Hills branch of the Manchester United Supporters Club like me. Or at least, I tried to head north but ended up back in the centre of town and staring at a yellow shipping container emblazoned with the recognisable branding of Bunsik, a fast-growing Korean fast-food chain known for its Korean corndogs, tteokbokki (spicy rice cakes), kimbap (rice rolls) and Korean fried chicken. Annoyed as I was at my poor navigating, I rolled my eyes at the inevitability of another chain concept roll-out and walked past, staring hard at the map on my phone so that I might make better progress towards Climat. Imagine my annoyance when, minutes later, I find myself approaching the same yellow Bunsik but from the other direction. Deciding there must be a reason I can't escape this popular Korean chain, I pop inside and order a corndog and a tiny portion of Buldak mayo fried chicken, just to give me pause to properly orientate myself, you understand. Sitting waiting for my order, I'm struck by the thought that, save for the branding and menu, this could be any McDonald's, Subway, KFC or Pizza Express, so typically British are the clientele – students huddled around backpacks sharing chips, tables of families, solo diners, couples, groups of friends giggling over social media videos and kids begging their parents for more. I'm astonished by the ease with which this broad demographic has embraced the relatively new Korean corndog concept as if it is a street food they grew up with, inherently part of their culinary culture. Except for most people here it isn't, much as Korean food is certainly one of the cuisines to have been increasingly adopted into our culinary lexicon, our supermarket aisles and our store-cupboards at home over the last decade. All of which goes to support my hypothesis that, by nature, Brits are curious and endlessly willing to try new things.

It's all very tasty, my dipped and dunked and fried treats, and before long I'm racing around the city with a renewed vigour.

Listen, Manchester is a marvel. Everyone is young and seems to have enough money to afford rent or a mortgage, to buy a coffee on their way to work, to eat out once or twice a month, to support local businesses. It seems, much like in Stockholm and Copenhagen and Berlin and Amsterdam, that you can live and work within the city limits, spend a minimal amount of time and money getting from home to work, and from what I can tell as I traipse about writing this nonsense in my head, everyone seems happy to be up here, making the most of a city that's on the up. Of course, I'm not so naive as to believe this is the whole truth. Manchester has benefited from regeneration over the past few decades, and its once sooty and industrial corners are primped and shiny. I can't ignore, though, as with any project of this ilk, that regeneration soon turns into gentrification, and that the poor saps who've spent decades rubbing along in a place they thought was perfectly good as it was are priced out of their neighbourhoods. And what, culinarily, is lost in this redevelopment? By now, I am walking through Ancoats, an old industrial area of Manchester known for its mills and once also called Little Italy, for all the Italian immigrants that moved to this part of the city in the nineteenth and early twentieth centuries – it is one of the areas that has been most radically transformed. And so we have Erst and Ruddies, two bleedingly trendy dining spots, as well as great Vietnamese sandwich spots and new-fangled yet authentic ramen, and I loudly record voice notes to myself about how this is a model for urban development that seems to keep young people and families in the city centre by providing everything they might need, and all the while I am ignoring what might have been lost. Of course, there are deep injustices at play when working people are pushed out of the centre to run-down suburbs, in order that young affluent office workers might replace them. I am worried about the little Italian restaurants and workers' cafés that will be lost to history. That said, gentrification is a nationwide phenomenon, and to a casual observer Manchester is a joy to behold, a city that seems to have rediscovered its joie de vivre. For me, though, as someone who is trying to document what British food is now, Manchester offers the same problems I discovered in Edinburgh. All the world is here and every iteration of every cuisine is catered for – so where do you start?

I end my time in Manchester in Mackie Mayor, a converted market hall filled with food vendors and craft breweries, the kind of place you'd see in any thriving European city. There is good food that uses local produce in joyful renditions of tacos, pizza, ramen, steak and chips, fried chicken and Thai, and a little bar is serving local beer, cider and abstract soft drinks. From what I could tell from my fellow punters, it's a place to come to catch up with mates, to grab a drink after running club, or to fill up on carbs if you're going out-out.

Sitting on a stool, staring at an exposed brick wall with a local craft beer and a couple of passable tacos about to land in front of me, it would be easy to hate everything about this place. The food is not top-drawer, more a good attempt at a thing, and the industrial-core aesthetic is decidedly unoriginal. The fact that you're supposed to order on an app can feel confusing and off-putting, but markets like these serve a purpose. I am here at the time of the day when the last of the daytime patrons mix with the first of the after-work-drinkers and the anxious early-for-dinner characters. There are trendy locals having tea with their kids, there are tourists loving the beams and exposed brick, there are craft beer obsessives rating a flight of thirds from the guest taps, and there are flirty couplings sizing each other up. It feels very British – and representative of a certain type of new gentrifying development in our urban centres. Ten years ago, I would have expected a market like this to have focused on bao buns, Israeli salads and ceviche; in ten years' time Mackie Mayor might be the go-to place for Somali street food, West African jollof, Filipino fast-casual options and a Palestinian Musakhan rôtisserie joint. The wise foodie might dismiss these places as part of the property-development-as-food culture trend, but like Cook and Lounges, what's on offer is a great reflection of what's new in British food for a certain engaged and food-loving audience.

Walking back to where I parked the car, I get a call from a friend who runs a hospitality tech business. Getting wind of the fact that I'm in one of his favourite cities to eat in, he excitedly spits the names of restaurants down the line at me, directing me to an Izakaya in the oldest railway pub in Eccles, a Nordic concept up a tower in the city centre, a live fire-cooking wine bar, a Michelin-starred cottage in the woods and an Indo-Chinese place in Burnage. The list goes on, and it is exciting to hear it unfurl. Yes, Crewe has suffered at the hands of dodgy franchise concepts, and Wilmslow caters to a crowd who want to breathe a bit of joy into a cold Cheshire evening by taking themselves to Santorini or Capri via their local high street, but there's so much here to love. Of all the places I've visited so far, the restaurants and food on offer in the north-west seem to represent the people who live there better than anywhere else.

The truth is, I am one man – and I am painfully aware of what I'm missing on this trip. The list I'm read over the phone might hint at the dishes and cuisines that will become part of our British diet in the next ten years, but for now, I feel confident that Manchester is a food mecca in its own right that competes with other major European cities more than it reflects what your typical British family up and down the country are having for their tea.

5

Wales

There are Italians in Wales – that much we know. And plenty of Welsh people too, of course. And the English. So many of the English. Of me, or us. Especially up north and down south, as we maraud over the border and play golf and use the supermarkets and enjoy the coastline. Sometimes we even move there.

I've spent time in the south, in Swansea and its environs, in Pembrokeshire, around and about Cardiff. I've been up north, too. Porthmadog, Portmeirion, Conwy. Where I'm headed now though, and where I'd like to focus for the foreseeable, is the middle of Wales, its belly button if you will, the centre of Wales's narrowest point, its cinched waist between Shropshire and Aberystwyth – a place called Llanidloes.

As I am discovering more and more as I whizz about Britain, a city can suggest things to you that a rural community will disprove in seconds. What city folk think of as normal, their countryside cousins will decree as madness – and vice versa. And I am still trying to make sense of who to believe. Bowl into the One Stop in Llanidloes and announce that what they, the locals, eat today has been inflected with the influence of the growing Polish and Romanian diasporas in Wales and they'll tell you that your collar must be done up so tight that it's cutting off circulation to your brain.

Welsh Wales is on the shrink, though. The death rate was higher than the birth rate in Wales in the last census. So the fact that the population continues to grow in Wales can only be due to net migration.

There are two Indian restaurants, one Bangladeshi restaurant, a Chinese takeaway, a Turkish kebab shop, a fish and chip shop, a British caff and a couple of tea rooms in Llanidloes. There's a Spar for your basics, a health food shop, a hempy whole-foods community-run organic-produce type shop for nice sourdough bread and muddy, leaves-on veg, and there's a very good butcher. For a supermarket you'll want the next town over, a twenty-five-minute drive away.

I thought I was being very clever choosing this mid-Wales town for the bulk of my research in Wales. As I drove over the border at Hay-on-Wye, I had bucolic images of a place that was embedded in its own rural customs and food traditions while also being influenced by the cosmopolitan university town of Aberystwyth forty minutes away on the coast and the southern cities of Cardiff and Swansea pushing upwards. Sadly, at first impressions, there was not a jot of that to be found.

Having arrived into Llanidloes in darkness, trundling up a long track and finally settling into the cottage that would house me for the week or so I'd be here, I had no food in the house, so the following morning I headed into Llanidloes proper to get some breakfast, get the lay of the land in terms of food culture and buy some supplies for my stay.

The aforementioned hempy food shop, or Great Oak Foods, to give it its proper title, had just received a delivery of what in London would have been considered Instagram-worthy bread and pastries, but here was simply considered Andy's Bread, which turned out to be utterly excellent. Andy, I learn, uses good flour, much of it milled very nearby (his wholemeal flour is grown and milled in neighbouring Ceredigion), to make good sourdough bread to sell locally to people who are grateful and delighted. It's a wonderful business model that means he is very popular around these parts but has no need or desire to be known any more than that. To put it more simply, he isn't massive on TikTok. What he is, though, is further proof that bread, bakeries and pastries are the one sub-genre of British food that is alive and thriving consistently across the UK.

We borrow, magpies ever, and we adapt – and Andy is no exception. There are baguettes, croissants, pains au chocolat and pains au raisin, pinched from the French; nice risen coiled buns with cinnamon and cardamom and vanilla, borrowed from the Scandis; pizzas and pillowy-topped focaccias yoinked from the Italians; and some good old loaves and schoolboy's-dream-filled doughnuts to round out the offering. At the other end of the high street is the Little Welsh bakery, a spot for a fine Welsh cake and a very good coffee. So both the expected and new and the traditions are cared for in the coffee and baked goods category here; all boxes ticked.

But what would have been here before Andy? Llanidloes is not a small town, it is old and once had money, so would have once supported a few bakeries – one for bread and savouries, perhaps, and one for sweet treats. What would have been on those counters? Delicious, European and Instagram-worthy as today's offerings might be, are they an improvement?

As luck would have it, Llanidloes has a bookshop that indexes very hard on both Llanidloes and Wales. It's easy to find a book on Welsh food, which goes some way to answer my own ponderings; I learn that a bakery in Llanidloes in the 1940s might have had a selection of traditional breads, a cottage loaf, a white loaf and a soda bread; it would have had some savouries, a meat pie, a sausage roll, a tray of faggots, cheese and onion turnovers, leek and potato pie; and it would have certainly had some sweeter bakes, too. Bara brith is a legendary local speciality, a fruited tea loaf where the fruits are soaked in tea before being used in the cake. To say nothing of Welsh cakes, also known as griddle cakes, bakestones or pics, those glorious flat little treats where sweet spices such as nutmeg, cinnamon and mixed spice are brought together with currants or sultanas in a small flatbread that's cooked on a griddle before being dusted in caster sugar. A miner's lunchbox classic, they almost died off when the mines closed, but the Welsh weren't going to let them go that easily; they're present in almost all the cafés and coffee shops I've visited in Wales. And let's not forget seed cake, a traditional loaf cake made using caraway, that often overlooked spice that combines a hint of aniseed with an earthy citrus sweetness and elevates the humble seed cake to a real treat. There would have been some form of scones, of course, and rock cakes, fruit buns and perhaps even a ginger cake. As a bakery counter goes, it doesn't sound bad; in the right hands, even now, it could be as enticing as the offering we often find. In Wales, traditional bakers tend to lean heavily on lard and dried fruit as opposed to butter and laminated pastry; the latter is perhaps a sexier upgrade, but it's hard to claim that we didn't have a distinct and enticing bakery culture back in the day. I wouldn't go as far as A. A. Gill in claiming the move from butter to olive oil did more damage to Britain than the Nazis, but I will say that we have lost something essential from Welsh – and therefore British – foods as we have lost the connections to our old bakery traditions. Our magpie tendencies are good at swapping the old for something new and shiny, but we could learn from the bird's hoarding tendency and hold on a little to what we have.

It is interesting to note that by the 1980s, items listed in the book as local and popular started to reflect influences from elsewhere. Cheese and tomato pizza slices, doughnuts, custard slices, cream horns and caramel slices point to a world that has embraced mass-produced confectionery products into the supply chain. And so the loss of traditional Welsh baked goods started more than forty-five years ago.

History lesson complete, coffee secured, bread bought and the butcher's about to be unburdened of many of its best cuts, I stopped at the Rose Café, a typical high-street caff that promises fried breakfasts. It is in such establishments that one can often get a sense of the first signs of new influences on local food culture – and thus the direction British food is headed. It might be the local pizza place with the Masala Pizza, or the fish and chip shop with a smoked sausage to be battered and fried, that gives clues to the cultures currently making an impact. And so it was that I settled into a plastic chair and reached for the laminated menu.

Here at the Rose Café, little influence from elsewhere has seeped in, sadly. The breakfasts are exclusively of the full English variety, without even any room for a bit of laverbread as a nod to this being Wales. On another day, when I wasn't on a quest to find new directions in British food, a full fry-up would have sated me, but today I was crestfallen. What hope and insight the baked goods and coffee had given me, the Rose seemed hell bent on whipping away.

I order a full English and try to enjoy it, but somehow the omission of laverbread rankles. On the one hand, why should they offer it? Its slimy, briny presence is no doubt completely unwelcome to most palates nowadays, but it would have been a staple alongside eggs in establishments like this for centuries. And it points to a personal frustration I have with the British palate, which if you'll indulge me I'd like to unpack.

We've allowed ourselves to become dulled to the extremes of taste. Where our grandparents would have eaten liver and kidneys relatively regularly, and bitter salad leaves, sharp marmalades and briny-mineral laverbread to balance things out, we now turn up our noses at these foods that sit on the extremes of our taste profiles. In Japan laverbread would be imbued with a reverence by generations old and young. Its lore would be passed from generation to generation, so too the skill of its harvest, its preparation and its use in dishes. Laverbread is seaweed. It is harvested, washed, boiled for a very long time and then pressed and packaged for your delectation. Almost no one produces their own nowadays, but in the right places it is easily purchased. It has a deep mineral flavour, a brininess and an earthy, umami-rich, spinach-like quality. On a breakfast such as mine, it would often be shaped into a patty, rolled in fine oats, fried in bacon fat and served alongside my eggs and bacon as a delicious contrast to the rest of the fatty richness on my plate. And to a more traditional palate, nothing could be more welcome – or more Welsh. Those ties, though, it seems, have been cut – at least in Llanidloes. My breakfast is very good all the same, but it could have been even better for the contrast of this old treat.

Momentarily restored and at peace with my breakfast, I walk a few doors down the high street to where the butcher sits proud in a hearty stone building that points to its importance in the town. Excited, I climb the short flight of heavy stone steps and enter what I assume will be a cathedral to Welsh meat, only for my emotional state to crumble. At an initial glance I see a counter laden with mediocre cuts of classic British fare without a scrap of lamb in sight. The winding track that links the big road with our hilltop cottage scythes through field after field of sheep. They roam free, they block the lane, they are the living embodiment of endless jokes about the Welsh. And yet here I am staring at a butcher's counter without a single piece of lamb. And worse still, nothing of interest to replace it.

'No lamb?' I ask of the friendly butcher, who meets my confused scowl with a sing-song: 'Can I help?'

'Rarely nowadays,' she says. 'It's a deal too dear for most here, week to week. We move a few racks over the weekends, a leg or two as well if they call ahead. There's just not much call for it during the week.'

'What are people after instead?' I ask, hopeful again of some exciting shift in food culture in these parts.

'Chicken, whole or breasts, mainly. Sausages and bacon too, mind. We do plenty of steaks and pork chops.'

The typical supermarket fodder, I think, disappointed as I am in my fellow home cooks.

'How times have changed,' I offer wistfully, increasingly comfortable playing the role of culinary anthropologist. 'How quickly has all that fallen away? Lamb being a bestseller?'

'Not overnight, but the last few years it's all dried up,' she says, keen for me to order something or move along, I sense. 'When I first started here you'd do a tonne of diced lamb over a weekend. Big bag of spuds and ten pounds of best lamb for many families on Friday. Lucky if we shift the same in mince or sausages now.'

Ever responsive to subliminal marketing and limited by what's on offer, I take twelve leek and apple sausages, a kilo of mince, a decent pork pie and a bag of potatoes and bid the friendly butcher goodbye. The minute I am out of her line of sight I note down her pearls of wisdom with regard to the changing face of Welsh butchery and continue my reconnaissance of the high street.

I have spent countless hours on this British culinary odyssey staring longingly into high-street restaurant windows to peer at menus, in the hope that I'll find the future of British food; hoping that typical high-street Cantonese Chinese spots will have a section of Fujian or Shandong cooking; praying that the local Indian takeaway is actually run by a Keralan or Kashmiri family; that a corner shop is run by Malaysians or Syrians or a family from Romania and that the counter might hold menu items from their home. Or indeed, equally exciting, that a local family still holds the key to a pub, shop, restaurant or market stall and is making and serving long-held local classics that would otherwise have died out years ago, or has taken the warp and weft of recent history on this little island and been guided by it, and their own tastes and peccadilloes, to arrive at a menu of treats that say something about how we eat.

Of course this doesn't often happen. Every high street in places such as this has shops selling food that an owner or a chef has decided to prepare for sale that day, and maybe the truth is these wares don't fit my world view, don't adhere to what I find delicious, don't reference the foods, culture and cuisines that I feel are present now on this isle, are influencing our food. But they don't. They're happy selling pre-packaged, bought-in sandwiches, pastries and the like, as they know they'll sell, especially as there is a dearth of other options, and so more often than not we survive on what is offered. And our high streets in towns aren't much better – between Greggs, Betfred and Nisa Local, choice is often limited to the point of extinction.

That now, on this very trip, a stop in a Tudor-beamed pub in Llanidloes sees a sandwich menu with cheese and pickle, ham and coleslaw and tuna mayonnaise, all served in par-baked baguettes and with pre-made slop brought from Bakes or a similar wholesaler to the catering industry, says so much for where our cuisine has landed, how it is decided upon, why it is stagnant and stultified. What we had is lost, what we have is less, what we should have – or might have – is kept from us by our lazy acceptance of a limiting framework.

With a slight sense of resignation, I peer through the window at the Llani kebab shop and almost turn away on autopilot, assuming that I'm not going to see what I really want to see – authentic Turkish cookery rather than the usual high-street kebab staples. In fact, I spot what looks like it could be genuine innovation in a modern British staple. This, it turns out, is where the future is happening in Wales. There's the typical chicken or lamb doner, the shish and the kofta too, and as so often now there are pizza, burger and fried chicken-based options as well, but among all of that is what locally are termed Sar Beni Pizzas – sarbeni or perhaps lahmacun, the thin and crispy spiced lamb flatbreads that are delicious when topped with a crunchy onion-heavy salad and wrapped up.

I order a couple, one plain, one topped with lamb kofte, and sit in the car and eat them while I plot my next move. I'd love this to be a moment of elation, the lifting of the dark cloud that has sat over British food for much of this trip. I'd love my recounting of that first bite to be transcendental and requiring a soundtrack of Gregorian chants. I'd love even for that bite to have been pleasant.

Alas, we don't always get what we want. Sadly, what was produced was not the lithe, burnished, slightly chewy treat one might expect from a lahmacun or lavash bread but the soft, barely browned base of a ready-to-roll supermarket pizza dough. While the lamb kofte was red-flecked with pul biber and smelled of garlic, cumin and mint, it was under-seasoned and wet where it might have been browned, salty and moreish. A few mouthfuls and the half-finished sar beni pizzas are rewrapped and popped into the storage compartment of the car door, the car's blowers are fired up to clear the meaty condensation that has accumulated on the windscreen, and I decide to drive to Newtown, as reports have reached me of an organic flavoured milk dispensing machine run by a big local dairy farm there. Now *that* piques my interest.

A few turns out of Llanidloes and on to the main road and it hits me. It doesn't matter that the sar beni weren't the best. Weren't even good. What matters is that they're there. And that the people of mid-Wales buy them, and in enough numbers to keep the place open and to keep them on the menu. There wasn't much evidence of a diverse community around this area of Wales beyond the Llani kebab shop, but this place is popular – and the next time I'm round this way I'll be sure to see what other innovations have followed in their footsteps.

All this, and my failure to find any of those wonderful-sounding Welsh bakery items in Llanidloes, adds to a theory I've been contemplating for some time now. It's true that we have let most of our own food traditions and food cultures dissipate and die. We have, historically, replaced them with cuisines and dishes from a specific period of largely post-war immigration, leaving us with British-centric Italian, Indian, Pakistani, Bangladeshi,

Turkish, Cantonese and broader Chinese, Caribbean, Thai and broader South East Asian dishes that, once adopted and adapted, we've decided we're quite happy with. More recent waves of immigration have had less of a culinary impact, although certain parts of certain cities have joyfully adopted Polish or Eritrean or Nigerian dishes, but what's often frustrating is the pattern repeating itself. A new wave of immigration, new communities, and a new set of dishes based on traditional dishes from that cuisine, but once again bent out of shape to appeal to a British audience. That's the sar beni pizza. I am certain that if a traditional sarbeni had been produced, it would find an even larger audience here and become a national classic. As it is, this bastardised version leaves one feeling a little flat.

There is a silver lining to this repeating pattern, and that is the second and third generations of these families who are now looking at what was done to their cuisine, the bending out of shape to suit the needs of others; they are not just bending it back, but reshaping it as something even more exciting, a more specific version of the cuisine of their parents. When this happens, we don't just have a very good south Indian restaurant, we have a new restaurant specialising in perfect idli, or in a Hyderabadi biryani or in simple, gossamer-thin dosa. The kebab shop in Llanidloes isn't there yet, but this iteration is making space for the next generation to do as much when the time is right.

In our major cities this plays out in restaurant concepts of every cuisine, and every dish within that cuisine imaginable. Places that seem laughably corporate are in fact a by-product of a wave of second-generation British immigrants, or perhaps even recent immigrants buoyed by a culture and a customer base already open to the charms of their cuisine, so that when a new 'authentic' version of that cuisine is presented to them they are primed to accept it unquestioningly.

To the foodie who is proud of standing at the precipice of the cutting edge, these places, these Dishooms and Comptoir Libanais, or Rosa's Thai and Wagamama, are cynical, confused and not authentic at all. And yet they are an undeniable progression from the first wave of the cuisines that landed here. And, alongside these thriving chains from elsewhere, what do we have that is thriving that might be termed traditionally British? Greggs? Pret? There's nothing in the realm of a sit-down fast casual chain – and maybe there shouldn't be. Maybe that's not how British food was designed to be enjoyed. But almost every other cuisine imaginable has a fast casual concept on the streets of London. Why not our own?

As I pull into Newtown, I am working through fast casual concepts for British classics, for shepherd's pie pop-ups, a Lancashire hotpot meets Chongqing hotpot supper club, or a Yorkshire pudding burrito stand. That last one already exists, though what it sells is evidence that it shouldn't. Maybe some things are best left as they are.

Wales

*

Newtown is a typical British town, in that it has more charity shops than anything else. It's also replete with the identikit mix of one home interiors shop owned by – and designed exclusively for – families that moved here from London, a Co-op that makes the eyes water with its prices of cupboard staples, a Londis or OneStop with a mind-bogglingly bizarre offering, a shuttered greengrocer's, a butcher's, a craft beer shop with the same meaty guy in the same washed-out black band t-shirt and the same beard as every one of these shops everywhere.

Newtown is a pleasant place, but offers little learning. It's a good place for an Anzac biscuit, another trusty delicacy that has somehow made its way from Australia and New Zealand in the back pocket of trendy third-wave baristas, who now farm regenerative millet and run coffee shops all over rural Britain. Anzac biccies are named for the Australia and New Zealand Army Corps, and the biscuits are made for Anzac Day – the Antipodean equivalent of Remembrance Sunday.

Before leaving Newtown there is the small matter of the milk-dispensing machine I was tipped off about. I have seen these machines in rural spots up and down the country, and I always hope their existence is linked to a growing customer base, allowing dairy farmers more control over their prices in the fight against supermarket dominance.

A few summers ago I was in Sicily, where I noticed that each town had a machine or two that allowed locals to roll up with a car boot full of empty bottles and fill them with still and sparkling spring water. Alongside these machines there was often a milk dispenser, and sometimes other machines too, doling out day-to-day groceries direct to the consumer. Often here the pitch is that it is good, fresh milk direct from the farm, sometimes with the added perk of being organic or even raw. In more rural spots you'll often find buckets filled with kale, potatoes, cabbage, eggs and even flowers next to milk machines – not a bad way to do a weekly shop.

Here in Newtown, in further proof that Welsh farmers know a good thing when they see it, the milk is also available in banana, strawberry and chocolate flavours. And popular they are, too, if the branded cups I keep seeing poking out of bins in the town are anything to go by. While an old-fashioned farmer's stall might fit better the image of a bucolic, wholesome Britain, I'd say these bottles of flavoured milk in Newtown speak to a foodie Britain keen to try a new thing, but keener still for that new thing to be simple, delicious and linked to a fair payday for the farmer. As it was, I had a rich, luscious chocolate milk that took me back to a childhood trip to a sweltering Portuguese beach and made my mouth water for a sugared doughnut. Luckily for me, the nearest Spar had a couple of stale doughnuts that softened up in the pocket of my down jacket. I stopped off near a waterfall at Cadair and enjoyed the doughnuts, the last of the chocolate milk the perfect thing to wash them down.

And so from Cadair I'm back on the road to Machynlleth, to arrive in Aberdyfi, a stolid seaside town that has both year-round locals as well as a thriving holidaying-Brits scene, before heading south and driving towards Aberystwyth to see what the home of one of Wales's oldest universities has to teach us about British food from a Welsh perspective.

Driving in Wales is just the business. A meandering road with views across a valley to a waterfall – and not a tourist attraction, but just the route. An impossibility of greens. A discombobulation of elevations. A shock of weaves that make you forget other humans are with you, and you can't imagine having to share this lilting vista with anyone else, least of all with other drivers. As it is, as my passenger through this mesmeric countryside, you end up having to remind me to keep my eyes on the road, perhaps to swerve to avoid the oncoming VW Golf, occasionally to elicit a stern brake so that schoolchildren might remain unscathed as they leave the school bus at the top of a track that no doubt leads to a hamlet that would make a tourist purr.

Eventually, another stunning drive peters out at sea level and delivers us to Aberdyfi (pronounced Aber-dove-ey), a seaside town that would be recognisable to anyone who has visited Aldeburgh, Holt, Deal or Whitby.

As seen from the car park in front of its long, sand-dune-backed promenade, Aberdyfi is a picture postcard. A row of Victorian terraced houses, all in the colours of a posh man's cords, all cut up and reimagined in some way to offer restaurants and shops at ground level, holiday lets and flats on the upper floors. As I crawl along looking for a parking spot, I spy within this technicolour parade a good-looking ice cream shop, a high-grade deli stuffed to the gunnels, a fish and chip shop, a pizza place, numerous cafés ranging from the greasy and pleasing to the trying-too-hard-on-square-crockery. Eventually I find a spot in the car park and I'm delighted to open my car door and find I've parked next to a Filipino family, three or four generations deep, enjoying foil-wrapped parcels of what looks like lechon, the brittle-skinned slow-cooked pork synonymous with Filipino cuisine, with rice and a julienned salad of carrot, cucumber and perhaps papaya. The family are wrapped up nicely against the wind but look enraptured by the food in the foil and polystyrene containers. They're celebrating a birthday, and the children all have Welsh accents. Not wanting to disturb, I don't butt in and ask for more details of their meal, nor their decision to spend the day in the car park in Aberdyfi, but their lunch looks splendid and I'm jealous.

My only sadness as I leave the car park to walk to the top of town, and then make a long trawl of every food outlet and shop along the high street, is that the food of the Filipino communities here, or throughout Wales, is yet to infiltrate into daily life. The fish and chip shop at the top of town is a case in point. It has succumbed to delicious influences from elsewhere: alongside the typical choices there's the Bombay Bad Boy burger, the Spicy Mexican Burger, veg samosas and fried calamari with tzatziki, to name just a handful of the items on the menu that are presumably quite popular around here. Curry sauce or gravy seem to be the immediate knee-jerk request from every customer ahead of me in the queue, a fact I attribute to Aberdyfi being on the same latitude as the Midlands, where the same request would be heard, and as many order the burgers and the Celtic pies as they do the classic haddock and chips. The haddock and chips were very good by the way, as were the mushy peas with plenty of vinegar.

After a stroll along the beach to walk off some of the chips before heading to Aberystwyth, I spent a happy half hour with an ice cream in hand. If you come to Aberdyfi, you've got to try the Aberdyfi Ice Cream company, who make exemplary ice cream using only the best Welsh milk; the cone of honey ice cream I tried worthy of a place on the Trafalgar Square plinth for the joy it brought me as I loitered on a wall, eavesdropping on the discussions of passers-by. Everyone seemed to be discussing meals just eaten, meals about to be eaten, shopping lists for meals they would eat that night, at the weekend, or when Dave, Cynthia and Rosemary finally arrived for their few days by the sea.

From this loitering I can report a few things. People are incensed by the prices of the expensive delis, but will also pop in to see what's on offer and come out with a bag of crisps, a piece of cheese, some cured meat, a tin of fish or a bottle of wine that they're excited to try. For those that refuse the deli point blank, the Costcutter is more than suitable for the same treatment. It should be said that in both the deli and the Costcutter, the only two shops where raw ingredients for cooking can be bought, as is repeated up and down the country, local produce proudly jostles for space alongside food from elsewhere: Spain, Italy, France and Greece in the case of the deli, Danone, Nestlé, GlaxoSmithKline and Unilever in the case of Costcutter. Although people are surely delighted to see the local produce, they still baulk at the prices.

'Think of the mark-up, only having to come down the road it is,' I heard someone say. 'They won't be wanting up at the Dairy, prices they charge.' And that was just on the street outside the Costcutter while I finished my ice cream.

No one is truly up in arms, of course; if they were press-ganged and asked for a true opinion, no doubt these same characters would express huge pride at the local produce available in the chiller cabinets of Costcutter in Aberdyfi. We love a moan, though, and we're certainly feeling the pinch as a nation, so our desire to support local farmers and buy local produce is sometimes directly and painfully at odds with our means to do so.

It's worth noting that for a place where 90 per cent of the land is used for agriculture, the value realised from Welsh land by individual farmers is the lowest of all four UK nations, while their reliance on subsidies sits at 67 per cent. Welsh livestock farmers are the worst remunerated livestock farmers in the UK, and Welsh dairy farmers earn an average annual income of £60,000 as opposed to the £90,000–£100,000 that English and Scottish dairy farmers bring in. These are income figures – not take-home pay – and feed and other costs have spiked in line with things in our lives after Brexit, Covid and global conflicts since 2020. All of which indicates why the butcher in Llanidloes didn't have much lamb to sell, and the shops in Newtown and elsewhere have not had as much wonderful local produce as I would find across the rest of the country. And without scale it's hard for small farms to achieve value, or to match supermarket prices. If we become more willing to spend where we can on produce that matters to us, then we can help create the market scale to incentivise farmers and local producers to create products for us. I am not naive about the broader socio-economic factors that are at play, but it certainly bears thought as I walk back to the car, sated and buoyed but not completely bowled over by my findings.

As so often I have found on these journeys, there is a touch of 'grandpa's favourite film on a Sunday afternoon' about much of the UK. There is a down-at-heel charm about the mix of poorly rendered old British classics and haphazardly reappropriated delights from 'abroad' – especially in seaside towns.

Back in the car park, the Filipino family are looking

sated; one grandparent is asleep in the front seat of their car and the rest are enjoying milky teas and a selection of nice-looking cakes. Plucking up the courage to ask what the cakes are and where they got them from, they tell me that they're enjoying a flan and a coconut cake, both homemade, and that the tea is sweetened with condensed milk, a common and delicious way to take tea in all sorts of places outside the UK, but a sweet treat that is yet to infiltrate into daily life here. There are some traditions that we will preserve at all costs, and tea is one of them.

You have to head inland to pick up the road down the coast to Aberystwyth. I'm barely fifteen miles from the university town as the crow flies, but over twice that because of my route circumnavigating the estuary dividing the two places, and a touch more again so that I can take the glorious coastal road from Ynyslas down.

I've been told that the fish and chips near the beach at Borth are stupendous, so there's an added incentive to make the extra detour to the coast, and I can confirm that while many would struggle to recommend anything called the Surrey – especially when it is housed on the ground floor of a dilapidated Victorian detached villa, sandwiched between a place that sells doughnuts fried in old oil and a café with sticky plastic tablecloths and the butter and jams in little plastic pots, and where the view from the shop is of the high, grey sea wall that protects the town from the Irish Sea – if you find yourself near Borth beach, the fish and chips at the Surrey are really pretty good.

This is not a chip shop with eyes on the future, but it does have old-school fish and chip shop nostalgic charm by the fryer-load. Here thick pieces of cod or plaice, the only two options aside from scampi, are fried in a good batter that becomes shatteringly crisp once it's out of the oil. The only concession to new-fangled food here comes in the form of a development likely carbon-dated to 1992 or 1993, when Southern Fried chicken was added to the menu. There were no other diners the day we rolled by, and the chap behind the counter could be described as reserved under polite questioning, so I have no idea how many customers opt for the rissole or fried roe over two pieces of fried chicken and chips, nor whether the locals prefer the cod or the plaice. What I can tell you is that the rissole is a joy to see; my grandfather used to add one of these flattened cakes made of chopped fish mixed with parsley and spices, then coated in breadcrumbs and fried, to his order – so too the fried roe, a delicacy that the bottarga-and-tarama fans of small plate restaurants in urban centres ought to try. The oil for the frying is clean and the fish stiff and fresh, and if I was taking a bracing walk along this stretch of coastline I'd stop here before taking my spoils up on to the sea wall to eat with a view of the mole-brown sea.

And so it is that finally, high on good grease and the hysteria of a long stretch spent behind the wheel on winding Welsh roads, I pull into Aberystwyth and park up in a spot between a big dark university building and the entrance to the pier. Here, all of what is good and bad about British food is present in one pirouette. There's more fish and chips everywhere, and some good old Italian ice cream vendors. To my back is a Turkish spot, and just behind that a little hole-in-the-wall fried chicken shop called Lip-Licking Fried Chicken; up the road is Hollywood Pizza and a great deli called Ultracomida that sells very good French, Spanish and Welsh cheeses and cured meats alongside wine, bread and other accompaniments to the aforementioned. To cap it all off, without moving my feet so much as an inch, but by completing my pirouette, I can take in two identikit Chinese takeaways, proudly side by side, the Seafront Palace and the Kam Sing. At first glance I cannot see an Indian restaurant, but I know there will be one nearby, and once I spot it I will have ticked off the central tenets of British restaurant food outside of the major urban areas in Britain today.

You'll be pleased to know that having secured some necessaries from Ultracomida, it was only a few paces before Light of Asia and the Rana's Kitchen heaved into view and my British High Street restaurant bingo card was complete. On the upside, a tip-off secured in Ultracomida points us towards Mama Fay's Caribbean restaurant as being one of the best local spots to eat and drink. So I head off in that direction, my belly full, but the thought of jerk pork and chicken, curried goat,

Wales

Ital stew, fried dumplings and fritters helping me feel like I could just about squeeze in a little extra.

And a little extra I did squeeze.

Full of Mama Fay's succour, it is tough to consider the rest of the food and drink available on the high street. But I'm committed, keen to keep exploring and hopefully work off some of the carbs from Mama Fay's. Unfortunately for my bloated and groaning stomach, I trawled the internet before my trip and have a list of three or four more places that seem highly rated locally. The first place the internet guides me to is a non-starter. Rated 4.8 on Google, this well-meaning café is everything that is wrong with food in the UK. Calling itself a bistro, I witness two plates of food coming from the kitchen and being cheerfully plonked in front of unsuspecting diners. One dish sees a supermarket flatbread topped with something hummus-related. On top of it sits a pile of pale limp 'Mediterranean' veg, which seems to include whole unpitted olives, peeled aubergine, yellow peppers and large half-moons of slick onion. There is wilting bag-salad on the side. A beat or two after it is delivered to its intended, I hear a call across the restaurant. 'Is it all meant to be cold?' The next plates that come from the kitchen hold two vegan hotdogs, atop which is a composite liquor containing sweetcorn, baked beans and chopped red peppers, all suspended in a mahogany-coloured gravy that is fast dissolving the bun housing the sausage. Alongside this are barely fried big fat chips and more bag-salad. I only know the details of this particulate dish as I overhear the poor diners who have been affronted with it asking each other what exactly is in the gravy. It is at this juncture that I cease all interest in the menu and make a quick escape. I can tell you that the menu promised treats like a buddha bowl, Swedish meatballs, Cornish pasty, fish and chips and a soba noodle bowl. I still sometimes wake up in a cold sweat imagining the barbarism of each of those dishes in this particular establishment.

From here, the internet suggests another well-regarded local haunt: the Bulgarian Kitchen. It's not a beauty of a place, with a lurid green exterior and a handful of heavy tables and old bentwood chairs inside, but it is here. Or at least it was there when I was there; it's since closed. But when I visited it made me feel hopeful about the future of British food. A small team were making traditional Bulgarian dishes, packed full of flavour and love, and the people of Aberystwyth were lapping it up. The place had plenty of punters on the day I swung by. Bulgarian cuisine is heavily influenced by Ottoman cuisine, so what we might recognise as typically Greek or Turkish dishes crop up in Bulgarian cooking too, albeit often by another name. Moussaka, kofta, shish, borek and ayran all feature here, as do salads of chopped tomatoes and cucumber, topped with crumbled white cheese, and thick yoghurt salad with grated cucumber. Knowing that the Bulgarian Kitchen is now closed, I can't help but wonder whether if they had opened with the same menu but with the dishes written with their Greek or Turkish names, it might still be gracing the high street of Aberystwyth.

I have another long drive ahead of me and want to break the back of it while I have enough pecker left, when I spot a sign for Y Gornel out of the corner of my eye as I'm trying to navigate the little roads to leave town.

All sanded floorboards, chalkboard menus and independently roasted coffee, this is a café that might just sum up all of British food, so I pull over and walk back for a look. Y Gornel is a little bit local, but not overtly. Produce comes from a relatively small catchment area, and the cakes and other sweet pastries are made here, or locally, and are very good indeed. The breakfast menu has all the hallmarks of a modern British offering. Some pancakes, porridge and granola, all of which borrow from the global flavour index that includes cinnamon, cardamom and vanilla – Scandinavia, the US and good old Britain. And of course there's a fry-up, the first I've had with laverbread. Here it is more sludgy pat than oatmeal-fried puck, but on a forkful of egg, toast and black pudding, it is a briny-earthy-umami kick that adds plenty to a mouthful. Rejoice.

For lunch there is a mix of quiches and curries, pasta, risotto and Spanish stews, a sandwich or two served with big chips, a salad and sometimes a cheeky jug of gravy. On top of this there is a traditional cawl, one of Wales's most iconic stews. The menu changes regularly, of course, but this is what I could observe, and it made me very happy indeed. The cawl especially warmed my heart, as it was handled with a modern but not reductive hand. At the end of this trip I'll have cawl in another café that is watery and insipid, all its deliciousness sucked out in a way that says: this is tradition and boo to you if you have any complaints. I won't mention that cawl again.

In modern Welsh, the word cawl (which rhymes with 'owl', not 'shawl') simply means 'soup', and the version you see on menus is more properly called *cawl Cymreig*, or Welsh soup. Tradition dictates that it should be made only of lamb and leeks – perhaps swede and potatoes too, at a stretch – but here the locals know that rules were made to be broken. Before Welsh branding movements ossified the recipe into a single, and often quite bland dish, cawl used to be made with beef and salted bacon and home cooks didn't bother with potato at all. Liberated from false tradition here, the beef is seasoned and browned and reduced to its jelly-wobbling best, while each vegetable is cooked just so and contained within a broth that has both heft and lightness, depth and a fleeting pleasure. That this sits alongside good pastas, sandwiches and Spanish stews on the menu, while feeling just as modern and reflective of the food Welsh people want to buy to eat for their lunch, is exciting.

Back in the car and ready to head inland again towards Llanidloes, I find myself wondering what food would once have sustained folk in these valleys. What might daily life have looked like? What have we lost? What improvements have come in its place? In the car I flick back through my little book of Welsh cookery, trying to write a menu of typical Welsh classics in the 80s. Faggots, mash and peas, minced beef and onion pie with chips and gravy, corned beef hash, liver and onions, steak and kidney pudding and Glamorgan sausages, those lovely little cheese and leek sausages rolled in oats and fried to perfection. It's a tempting bill of fare, but I can see why most of it has lost its popularity. It'd be a one-dimensional diet in its richness, for a start, although you can see how such a menu might have helped prop up livestock farming.

So the broadening choice of dishes on offer here hasn't improved the lot of farmers, that's for sure. And with more restaurants nowadays than ever before, more people eating out, travelling for holidays and buying cookbooks for cuisines that their ancestors wouldn't have had a clue about, I still wonder if our high-street offering in places such as this might be better. There is hope, though. When a spot like Y Gornel gets it right, the British diet offers, or reflects, an exciting future. And when a nice deli offers local Welsh charcuterie, or Ultracomida has the best Welsh cheese side by side with our favourites from France, Italy and Spain, or when local honey and delicious Welsh milk gives you an ice cream worth travelling the country for, it suggests a simmering pot of British food that might just reach a rolling boil sometime soon.

Wales has shown me that we're a nation of extreme highs, one-hit wonders and moments of transcendental joy that showcase everything good about a cook, an area and its produce. But there are also lows, businesses with the heart ripped out of them by the misplaced perception that they need to modernise in order to draw a crowd and make enough cash each month to cover their ever-increasing rents, rates and wages. Systemic changes could help, but so too could a changing of the economic wind; with a little more cash in our pockets we could use our spending power to fan the flames of a burgeoning local producer- and farmer-led revolution, the shoots of which are present all across the country. Thus the best of what I've found would thrive, and the mediocre might give way to more opportunities for the good stuff. Perhaps a new Filipino spot or two? I know I'd drive out here for lechon; I might even plan a holiday around it.

6

The West Midlands

During my formative years as a chef, I worked almost exclusively with chefs from Birmingham. Stevie Parle, who owns Town on Drury Lane and previously ran Dock Kitchen in Ladbroke Grove, where I trained as a chef, grew up just outside Birmingham, as did Alex Jackson, Stevie's head chef, who went on to own Sardine, and be the head chef at Noble Rot Soho and the café at Leila's Shop in Shoreditch. Stevie's sister Lizzie ran cult café Railroad and was head baker at E5 in Hackney. One step removed from my immediate colleagues was Ben Chapman, who runs such heralded establishments as Smoking Goat, Kiln, Brat and Mountain in London, and is also from Birmingham.

My point is that I've long associated Birmingham with good, forward-thinking food – and that was before I'd seen Glynn Purnell and Aktar Islam on *The Great British Menu* or knew about April Bloomfield, who trained at the River Café before becoming one of Birmingham's most successful culinary exports, taking her extraordinary cooking to the Spotted Pig, the Breslin and now Sailor in New York.

On top of my personal association of Birmingham with people who are expert at cooking nice food, I'm acutely aware of the city's Balti Triangle and its demographic makeup and large number of first- or second-generation immigrants from Pakistan, India and Bangladesh; 31 per cent of its population describe themselves as of Asian descent, with 11 per cent describing themselves as being of Black and of African or Caribbean descent. Both these facts have always suggested good food to me. The presence in Birmingham of the Cadbury chocolate factory on the one hand and Island Delights, the largest Jamaican patty producer in the UK, on the other, has also struck me as indicating a place where they have an eye for a good thing when they see it. The fact that the city is home to both the most popular chocolate business and our biggest patty maker is a sign, I suspect, that I will uncover more delights as I venture deeper into the city.

All this means I'm more excited about travelling to Birmingham than almost anywhere else on this trip. Surely this is a place where we might get a sense of what a new British menu might look like?

And so it is that I unintentionally find myself in Becketts Farm Shop in Wythall, just off the A435, having programmed my sat nav to take me to King's Heath, a student stronghold to the south of the city centre. I feel giddy as I stand in a queue in front of a counter displaying the fattiest roasted meats I've ever seen and try surreptitiously to photograph the extraordinary displays of curry sauces, chutneys, perfectly iced cakes, pies and biscuits – some from the traditional tea-dunking end of the spectrum, others from the soaked-in-syrup-and-bejewelled-in-pistachio-or-rose-petal variety, and everything in between.

I've spotted a tray of faggots, brought out from the back, the dark orbs of minced offcuts and offal mixed with herbs and wrapped in perfectly rendered and browned caul fat, a thin, lace-like membrane surrounding them. As they pass by, I'm mesmerised by the juices lapping in the tray. I have a personal history with faggots. Something in their offally nature has always drawn me to them, even as a child.

I recall one school trip to Normandy when I was about ten. We were probably there on a history trip, but all I can recall is being offered andouille de Vire, a coarse local sausage made from pig intestines and seasoned with sea salt. In my memory, everyone – the cook, the waiter, local guides, other diners in the roadside gîte – was dismayed when I insisted that I'd love to try this speciality. I must admit, it was bloody-minded stubbornness that stopped me bolting from the table and vomiting in the nearest bin when the thing was placed in front of me, but it is with pride for my ten-year-old self that I recall taking a morsel and popping it into my mouth. As with many stinky foods, the bark is always worse than the bite. This was actually bloody good, an umami explosion, sweet and rich but with a sour, offally meatiness that as an adult I still crave a couple of times a year.

Anyway, the point of this rambling anecdote is to highlight the reverence in which this dish was held in France – and to compare it to the indifference such magical treats receive here. Faggots should be a national treasure; we should have festivals in the Midlands in their honour, and yet we reduce them to a sneered-at niche and fail to imbue them with any reverence whatsoever.

Queuing now at the service counter, I am surrounded by builders, some retirees and a couple of groups of office workers. Everyone is ordering baps, filled with all sorts. A burly chap ahead of me is getting some delicious-looking bright-red-coated meat, sliced and piled as high as the filling in a Katz's Deli sandwich. I'm guessing it's tikka-spiced chicken or turkey breast, and yet he seems to be topping it with apple sauce and cheese. Others are dedicated to slices of soft pork with crackling, apple sauce and mushy peas. By now my eyes are focused on the mahogany faggots while I try to decide whether I should ask for a bap or a bun. Bap is what most are saying, although one of the office workers asked for a roll without being mocked. They had a Brummie accent though, and mine is at best southern, at worst posh – either way, nothing like the accents of the other customers. I know that in these parts a bun or roll is most likely called a bap – perhaps a cob, but my understanding is that would be more common in the East Midlands, while barm is used further north. As I'm inching closer to the server with the tray, I still can't quite recall what is what. Bap sounds wrong, but that's the most common word I'm hearing – and the idea of putting on a Brummie accent and asking for a faggot bap seems easier than talking in my normal voice.

'Owl right?' the server says.

'Yes thanks,' I mumble, my accent posher than I was hoping for. 'I've got myself in a pickle about bread rolls. It's a bap in these parts, right?'

'Aye, bap or cob – up to you.'

'The faggots look good.'

'Bostin.'

I'm on shaky ground.

'A faggot bap, then, please.'

'Peas?'

I pause, certain I've already said please.

'Please,' I offer again, as a ladle of mushy peas is added to my faggot-filled roll.

'Thank you,' I enunciate, overdoing my enthusiasm.

'Next,' the server barks over my shoulder.

I tuck into the soft bun and immediately feel sad. Flat, fatty, flavourless. The perfect texture for someone with dentures to gum their way through, but not a pleasing thing. But how? The dark matter of a pig, minced and rolled and seasoned with salt and pepper and perhaps a tickle from mace or allspice, and wrapped in fat and braised hard in a dark gravy. How can that not taste of much? I fear my clumsy ordering might have meant missing out on the offer of extra salt and vinegar, for that is what this needs, but still. Suddenly the lad with the turkey-tikka sandwich seems hardwired into a British culinary future in a way that I'm clearly not.

Lesson learned, I get back on the road to King's Heath, where cool cafés, good coffee, new-wave pizza and a backstreet Korean spot all await me. Having found a parking space, I take my notebook and head south on the high street with the intention of completing a stroll of the main thoroughfare, to get a sense of the place and the food that's on offer on the outskirts of Birmingham.

We're four miles out from the city centre proper, and the place has the feel of a village. Not a bucolic one, you understand – there's no mill pond, no village green, and you're well aware that this is a main artery into the city centre – but there is a sense that this is its own place, that it has an identity. A mix of students, young parents with buggies, people going about their daily business who seem passionate about where they live.

And the population of King's Heath is young – a quick search suggests the vast majority are forty-four and under, with nearly a quarter being under eighteen. So this is a family place. The comedian Joe Lycett put the place on the map when he applied for King's Heath to be an official 'gayborhood', and he has hosted King's Heath Pride every year since 2021; this is not a stuffy, traditional or parochial place – it is full of engaged young people, and it doesn't have to pander to tourists or holiday-makers. I sense this as I walk up and down and around. And I begin to feel that King's Heath might be a place with answers – that it might hold a clue as to what British food is.

Buoyed by this thought, I skip into a café that looks the business, where a good mix of locals are all eating and drinking and looking very happy indeed. The aesthetic is Scandi-chic-meets-British-upcycling; there's a bleached plywood counter with some pastries and a low shelf behind the counter piled with trendy bags of coffee, yet the vibe is not introspective or self-consciously cool. I'm greeted by a warm hello and find an empty table between a couple discussing home renovations and a pair of grandparents looking after their granddaughter. There are some freelancers dotted at laptops, and a group of nurses come in for takeaway coffees and giggle themselves into a round of cinnamon buns too. Over in the corner, two friends speaking Arabic seem to be having an English lesson with a Greek woman who, it becomes apparent, works in the café.

This place is not really one thing or another. It would not trouble a food reviewer and none of the food is particularly praiseworthy. In fact, my cheese toastie is actively unpleasant, run through as it is with roasted broccoli, lingering truffle and some inexplicable braised red cabbage. If I were a restaurant critic the food would make my blood boil; someone here must hate me, I'd conclude, to commit such a crime with what would in the right hands be simple, delicious comfort food. Thank God, then, that I'm not a restaurant critic, but this hateful cheese toastie does tell me something about why British food is often so dire – about how we throw delicious or trendy ingredients together in the name of menu creation, without much care for whether it really makes the best of each thing.

I lived in a flat once with a woman who was very nice but also the strangest person I've ever had to witness putting together a plate of food. For her there were no red lines. No combinations of texture, temperature or taste that couldn't end up together in one dish. Leftovers would be unceremoniously emptied on to a plate, destined for the microwave; something with salad, avocado or cucumber might be nuked alongside a rich stew, a few types of carbohydrate, perhaps together with a dressing or mayonnaise and often a pickle, coleslaw or chutney too. Once everything had been merrily microwaved, the hot cucumber and split sauces would be mixed into the rice and potato and steamed fish and pork belly, for instance, and the pile of competing flavours would be eaten with audible pleasure. I stopped eating at the same time as her, preferring to think of her as the intellectual powerhouse she was as opposed to the base savage that her meals indicated. The fascinating thing though is that once, when I was drunk at a wedding, I asked her about her bin-bottom-buffet technique. And to my shock, she started waxing lyrical about chefs and restaurants like Ottolenghi and Honey

& Co – it seemed that she engaged in and took pleasure from good recipe writing. So why didn't she know better? Because she had taken an array of recipes and culinary knowledge from cultures and traditions with very different styles of cooking, and mistaken the act of combining small plates of complimentary flavours for an invitation to create a mezze plate from any leftover, and in any form.

And this sandwich was telling me something similar about British food culture. In among the leeks, soggy broccoli and braised red cabbage were flavours that might have been described as Middle Eastern. Some cumin, lemon juice or sumac, perhaps a bit of za'atar or chilli. These spices had been used to mask the gaseous hum of overcooked vegetables and brought to the sandwich alongside synthetic truffle oil, melted cheese and bacon. It's a good example of how even an engaged cook can draw the wrong conclusions from a wonderful set of inputs. And more frequently than we'd like to admit, that is what much of British food has become.

I've come across similar mash-ups everywhere, but the crucial point is that while we have rejected the stultifying traditions of jams, pies and stews, instead embracing new cuisines, when we've tried to let those foods seep into our own, we've invariably made a mess of the coupling. There have been some successes, quite often visible in sausage roll and Scotch egg fillings, things like lamb and harissa or chorizo and apple, but most of these hybrids – my cheese toastie included – are failed experiments. From this frustration, I hope, the future of British food will emerge.

At the moment, all I can feel is that, left alone for long enough with Italian ragù, Indian curry, Chinese stir-fries, Jamaican stews and Nigerian rice, we've invariably made things worse. If we compare this with what other cultures have done with our dropped crumbs, with tins of luncheon meat and processed cheese, or with our pies and stews, we can see what we could have achieved if we just cared a bit more. Contemporary dishes across the world owe much to the detritus the West left behind once we were finished fighting or colonising in their lands. Things like Macanese custard tarts or curry beef brisket, a Hong Kong café staple that owes much to British colonial trade routes and the incorporation of South Asian curry powders. Or Spam Kimbap in Korea, a twist on the traditional rice roll that replaces classic proteins such as fish or seafood with slices of Spam. Or Japan's curry rice, introduced by the British Navy during the Meiji era, adapted from Indian curry powder and transformed into one of Japan's most beloved comfort foods. And I think we all know the origin story of banh mi by now, too.

Over half my toasted sandwich remains untouched. I leave cash, including a generous tip, put my headphones in and make for the door. Out on the high street, wondering how long the synthetic truffle flavour will linger on the back of my tongue, I decide to move on. I plan to come back to try the Korean spot I've been recommended, and the pizza place that the internet seems to love looks promising. For now I continue towards Birmingham proper, and its Bullring, indoor market and Balti Triangle.

The last time I was in Birmingham proper I recall my Brummie chef friends recommending a place where the back of the Bullring, the edge of the indoor market and a three-storey pan-Asian food hall meet. Foot traffic brings with it opportunity, and thus opportunists in the form of traders, some selling knock-off underwear and some selling food. And so, with the synthetic truffle oil taste still lingering, I drive straight into the centre of Birmingham and park right where these three local behemoths converge, ready for a proper look at what the multicultural cross-pollinating forces in this area might tell us about the state of British food.

Out of the car, I survey the raging river of concrete that runs ahead of me. The three-storey office block that houses Asia Asia is behind me, the entrance to the indoor market to my right and the steps up to the back of the Bullring to my left. The success of Kirkgate Market in Leeds still in my mind, I decide that the indoor market looks more promising than the big shiny Bullring shopping centre, so I cross the road, heave open a door and step into an atmosphere laced with the copper scent of animal blood and the distant hum of stockfish hanging in a chiller.

'Snore! Prices are prices. You wouldn't haggle with the label in a supermarket, would you love?'

Two elderly East Asian women talk among themselves, clearly not new to the charming patter of the British fishmonger in front of them, their standard issue shopping trolleys gripped tight in defence. I don't hear their reply as I'm pretending to browse the nearby stalls, but it's hardly a charming introduction to the place – a fact not helped by the clear demise of this market, as judged by three of the five stalls in the small section I've arrived in being closed.

As I voyage deeper into the belly of the market, I observe a mixture of British fare, West African grocers and beauty shops, Caribbean grocers, Asian grocers and a few Middle Eastern shops selling sweet treats, spices and nuts. Despite the liveliness of the stalls, it's hard to ignore that the majority of stalls are not open; some are seemingly abandoned, plastic sheeting thrown over stock, shutters down and locked, while others are completely bare.

A market like this needs energy to survive. They exist up and down the country, at either end of the class spectrum. I've visited them in Leeds, Canterbury, Tebay and somewhere off the A303 and marvelled at the joyful churn of custom. The best of this sort of market I've ever found was in Mexico, where an entire micro-economy means that meat sold can be cooked nearby, and if accompaniments and condiments are needed for a food stall, some savvy trader will supply the demand. Mexico might seem a long way from Birmingham, but markets I've visited in Amsterdam, Madrid and

Stockholm have all achieved this ecosystem, the effect of which makes a market hum. Here the market is dying. I make a couple of laps, hoping I might have missed the epicentre on my first pass, a mistake I made in a wonderful market in Madeira, when I discovered that I'd missed an extraordinary fruit and veg area housed in an adjacent building – and a fish market to rival anywhere in the world at the back of the building where I'd been browsing. I had not made the same mistake here. The indoor market in Birmingham is devoid of joy and energy.

Feeling deflated, I head back outside and stand among the thrum of pedestrians going about their business. I find a bench and consider whether the indoor market is in a transition phase. It is clear that the British fishmongers still do enough trade to just about survive, but it's also clear that they're not exactly thriving.

Where old-fashioned markets begin to wane, there is an opportunity for diaspora communities to take advantage of low rents and serve their communities from a central location. That said, it is clear that these stalls are by the diaspora, for the diaspora. Little cross-pollination is in evidence, if the store choices and purchasing patterns of the shoppers I observe today are typical. Not that this is a big issue. It is essential that these shops are here; it is just a shame that the market around them isn't thriving to the extent that customers are benefiting from the juxtaposition of traders. Perhaps I'm a generation early, I scrawl in my notebook; maybe we'll eventually see the trickle-down of the foods on sale here into households across the country.

Standing in direct contrast to the indoor market is Asia Asia, a three-floor food market in which traders take ownership of a small stall with a small kitchen and a counter at the front. Not a new concept, but one that at least has an energy here that's hard to ignore. I work my way up floor by floor, groups of diners all around me weighing up menu after menu, not wanting to commit to the wrong thing. The offering is broad but recognisable – a few Taiwanese spots offering their versions of bao, a few Korean kiosks offering fried treats or some twist on tteokbokki, a Japanese place selling ramen and udon and another selling sushi, a couple of Chinese spots and an Indonesian place with big bowls of creamy-looking laksa, the pictures on the menu showing pools of bright red chilli oil on top of most options.

Having completed a few laps, I plump for a bowl of laksa, some fried chicken, a few bao and some cheesy tteokbokki. At each place I'm given a black box that I'm assured will vibrate when my food is ready. I find a spot at a counter overlooking the market opposite, line up my vibrating boxes and wait. While I wait, I observe families filling tables and groups of students making the most of both choice and value; there are people on dates, as well as office workers taking a day off from having a meal deal at their desks. It feels hopeful, exciting.

The West Midlands

My boxes go off all at once – maximum vibration. The counter in front of me sends up a cacophony, two of the boxes falling off the edge of the counter and pinging off the metal stools as they hurtle floorward. One breaks in two, its wires and batteries splayed, its ability to vibrate unaffected.

I gather my boxes and go to the counters one by one, a charade playing out at each place as I try to match the pager to the outlet. This debacle over, I return to my seat and marvel at the future before me, the bounty from which our new British menu might be composed. Feeling genuinely hopeful for the second time today, I lift a fried chicken bao to my mouth, take a bite and stop. The sticky bao have coated the roof of my mouth, and I can feel my frustration boiling when what I really need to do is masticate and breathe. I take a little ladle of laksa, hoping its rich coconut broth will soothe my mood and help rinse the bao paste filling my mouth. It is acrid with chilli oil and a hit of loo-cleaner citrus, causing me to splutter, my mind seething at its inauthenticity. Feeling duped, I look around again – and suddenly the other diners look disgruntled and bored where moments ago they nattered with a joyful hum. I'm reminded of the time I realised that the Buffalo Bill's Wild West dinner at Disneyland Paris was not a real-life display of touring cowboys but a slapdash dinner maximised for profit while a horse-fuelled circus entertained for an hour. I contemplate upping and leaving, my disappointment heightened by my embarrassment at the scene I've caused. I take a breath and a sip of brown sugar bubble tea. I look out at the concrete concourse, a pedestrian spaghetti junction. I don't want to venture out there just yet. I take a forkful of tteokbokki and let its fiery heat, its tomato soup richness, its TikTok-worthy cheese pull take me away from here, away from these people wondering why I've bought so much food and why I'm causing such a scene. My mouth full, I sink my teeth into the firm little rice cakes and all is forgiven. This is very tasty. I try a piece of fried chicken. The coating is crispy, as if it's been dredged, floured and battered twice over. It has layers that a chiropodist would have a field day with, so gnarled and brittle are the crags and lesions between skin and bone. And inside, flavour. Chicken that has been seasoned and then some. Returning to the laksa now, all is well. Even the bao seem to have softened.

Unable to eat everything I've ordered, I ask for the remainders to be boxed up, hoping that my hotel room might have the facilities to reheat these for a midnight snack later. As I wait for the boxed goods to be returned to me, I wonder whether it matters how good this food is, whether the authenticity of the experience is important. Although this food isn't as good as it could be, at least it's here.

Korean, Taiwanese and Indonesian food was not available to me growing up. My vision of British fare in the 1990s and early 2000s included French, Italian and Spanish food, curry, stir-fries and some Tex-Mex.

The West Midlands

The breadth of my cooking as a young adult started to stretch further, including regional Chinese knowledge spurred on by Fuchsia Dunlop and an exploration of Thai and Vietnamese food, Japanese food as evidenced by an obsession with *Masterchef* contestant Tim Anderson, Middle Eastern food thanks to Claudia Roden, Sam and Sam Clark and Ottolenghi. As a chef, my own journey went deeper; David Thompson introduced regional Thai food to my lexicon, Diana Kennedy drove me deeper into Mexico. And as my personal voyage of discovery gathered pace, so the British menu started to include things like chipotle, tomatillo and birria, sumac, za'atar and Szechuan peppercorns, lamb fat skewers and hand-pulled noodles. And some of these things ended up in people's spice racks and cupboards. And so, even though some of it is a slightly tame imitation of the real thing, the fact that Asia Asia is here and serving not just the standard British Asian foods but instead things from our extended culinary vision of that continent is exciting. It points to the new British menu I am searching for.

On the way to check in at my hotel, I pop into a city centre Sainsbury's. Sure enough, even in a small branch like this, I find gochujang, laksa paste, little vacuum-packed rice cakes and peanut milk. I even find bao in the freezer section.

Ensconced in my hotel room for the night, I pop my tower of takeaway containers into the mini fridge and decide to have a shower before dinner at Shabab's, a

Birmingham institution with credentials as ironclad you could hope for, being one of the last remaining traditional balti houses still operating in the Balti Triangle.

Standing under the woefully underpowered shower listening through the paper-thin walls to a management consultant in the neighbouring bathroom loudly recounting the finer points of some dull manufacturing business, I am struck by the Asian section in that city centre Sainsbury's. In stark contrast to the 'farm shop' I stopped off at on the way into Birmingham, Sainsbury's 'foreign foods' sections do reflect the local diaspora and cultures of the area. For me, moving across South London, from east to west, meant leaving behind the West African, Chinese, Polish and Caribbean foods I could select from in the huge Sydenham Sainsbury's and instead undertaking a voyage of discovery that the Kingston branch presented with Korean, Turkish, Indian and Japanese treats. Of course, any self-respecting cook will plunder the unfamiliar aisles of the independent food shops that pop up when a diaspora community is established in an area, but supermarket foreign food sections retain a significant place in my toolkit.

My shower over, I am coiffed, perfumed and present outside my hotel ready to meet a friend who works locally, and who will be my dining companion for this journey into the Balti Triangle, a place with which I have a mythological fascination. We meet, greet and climb into the back of a worse-for-wear Uber, and start our journey to Ladypool Road, south of the city centre and at the top edge of the triangle of roads between Balsall Heath and Sparkhill that make up the triangle. The balti houses that used to line the streets are largely closed now, their demise a slight mystery, but linked in various theories to a correlation with pub closures, to a shifting demographic in the area – and to shifting tastes, away from the rich and the heavy and towards lighter cuisines.

Most reports suggest that only four traditional balti houses are left, and the ones that remain do a roaring trade both to tourists and to the local community, which includes one of the largest Pakistani Kashmiri populations in Britain – and the original kickstarters of the 1970s balti craze that reached a fever pitch in the 1990s and 2000s.

So where to start with balti? It's unique to Birmingham, and its history is the perfect lens through which to view the communities making their homes in the UK today.

This dish of balti is a specific thing – and like a tagine, the thing a dish is cooked in is also its commonplace name; a balti is a carbon steel bowl that is bashed out thin, with two little handles. The curry is cooked and served in this vessel, which gives it its signature deep flavour. It gets hot quickly, and the dishes are cooked in this searing heat, meaning a depth of char and flavour, and an end sauce with a rich darkness and depth.

Shabab's is one of the few remaining 'original' balti

houses. It is not as old as the dish itself, having opened in 1987, but the owner's uncle was one of the original balti chefs in the country, hence Shabab's tag line: 'Home of the Birmingham Balti'. Shabab's suffered a fire in early 2025, since my visit, but when I was there it had all the pleasing hallmarks of a traditional balti house: dark walls, waiters in starched black attire but with lightning-quick service, a menu listing an unending variation of baltis, alongside rogan josh, dhansak, dopiasa, bhuna and jalfrezi of every iteration. I soon discover that there are naans the size of the table, and every possible dhal and chutney you could imagine. I feel caught in limbo as we are shown to our table and the enormous menus are presented to us under the glass of the tabletop, reminded of a trope in *Ramsay's Kitchen Nightmares* where any overly long menu was presented as a sign that a restaurant was out of control. Aware of the balti house's demise, I can't help worrying that an ever-growing range might signify an attempt to please everyone, a route to failure. I park that thought, though, as I see sizzling baltis being carried to other tables, and as I clock my first expansive naan landing nearby, excitement replaces sadness. Our order sticks to baltis – one chicken, one lamb – lady fingers (or okra) and one king prawn and aloo. We also order a plain naan, rice, onion salad, raita and chutneys. And once all the food is collected around us, a couple of salted lassis to wash it all down, it's a pleasing sight. In its immediate aftermath, though, I realise that the balti represents a heavy and rich corner of Pakistani or Kashmiri food; even for a glutton like me, the meal sits heavy in the stomach long after its consumption.

I don't want to appear overly negative; it was delicious, and the Balti Triangle must be celebrated – and kept alive. That this corner of Birmingham was once a thriving community of like-minded Kashmiri restaurateurs is important. They were using a traditional cooking method, creating a new cuisine seen as modern and clever in its time, and aimed at luring a new audience; it was rightly celebrated as a fresh take on a traditional staple. Balti was a very British phenomenon while being very much of Birmingham – and very much Pakistani. Viewed through today's lens, it feels a little tired and overly rich, perhaps out of step with more modern tastes and lifestyles. It is no surprise that as we have become more concerned with health in our dining habits, we have gravitated towards Asian cuisines that favour coconut, fish and lime, whether Sri Lankan, Goan, Thai or Indonesian. Their rise is in direct correlation with balti's demise. And there have been sociocultural changes in the area; the empty units in the Balti Triangle increasingly being filled by Middle Eastern restaurants that reflect more recent local demographic shifts. Similarly, Korean restaurants, Thai places and South Indian food such as thali and dosas have taken hold – just as they have across the UK. Pizza places, burgers, small plates restaurants and food pubs are all now also present in the little area that once housed thirty-plus balti restaurants.

So the Balti Triangle, perhaps, is not the depressed story that some think. New communities moved into the void left behind by incumbent communities gravitating elsewhere; the net result is new businesses reflecting new cuisines, which will no doubt result in all manner of hybrids. Let's hope they replicate the balti craze – and that the traders in Asia Asia keep improving their fare. What the new thing will be is not yet apparent, but as I leave Shabab's and take an evening stroll around the streets surrounding the restaurant, it's out here, just waiting to cause a stir.

7

The South-West

Having left the Midlands, I decide to take on the long drive to Cornwall in one hit. It means forgoing the Cotswolds, and in doing so missing out on making pithy comments about Jeremy Clarkson's Diddly Squat Farm Shop and everything that might suggest about British tastes and choices. And Carole Bamford's Daylesford Farm Shop, and Soho Farmhouse too. Diddly Squat would suggest a sepia-hewn vision of a lost Britain, I suspect, just with more puerile jokes as part of its branding. And the other two are likely very pleasant indeed, although in some ways no different, in terms of what I might learn by stopping there, from reading the Cook brochure or a menu at Lounges, just a little more expensive I suspect. I whistle past Bristol and Bath too – Bristol in particular I am torn about skirting, but needs must and the tip of Cornwall is calling. I am but one man with a tight itinerary.

And so, having driven until late the night before, arriving in the pitch black, to enter Porthleven during the town's annual raft race, when locals use duct tape and plastic barrels to cross the harbour in fancy dress without sinking, is to step into a fever dream that might be overwhelming to some, takes me a moment to make sense of, but looks like a right laugh for those partaking. This is a jamboree; families in hoodies and Barbours and knee-length stripy socks and collar-up rugby shirts, with dogs on leads or on the end of surfboard bungee ropes, are playing out a typical British holiday around the harbour's horseshoe. It could be a Beryl Cook painting, with added Gore-Tex.

Salvation comes in the shape of a coffee shop, one of Porthleven's proudest institutions: Origin. A coffee roaster that began in this very village, Origin now dominates the 'specialist' coffee landscape in London and was one of the first to champion organic, fairtrade coffees, which means caring how the coffee is produced and tastes, as opposed to serving coffee to the masses that tastes more like hot tar mixed with water. Anyway, we all queue in blissful reverie, the scene across the harbour becoming ever more calming as the prospect of a fruity Peruvian filter coffee and a mahogany-glazed croissant gets closer. As I've already mentioned, the previous sentence might now read as Pure Britannia; nothing suggests a more British start to the day than a delicious, well-sourced and skilfully pulled coffee and a croissant, laminated and baked in-house. We don't speak to one another as we wait in line. Someone overly friendly tries to start a conversation about dark clouds on the horizon, but like wet kindling the queue won't ignite.

The South-West

And so we stand in silence and watch a calamity unfolding on the water. A Vauxhall Insignia is attempting to tow a pirate ship made of apple crates and black crêpe paper into the water, from where it will be boarded by paddle-wielding, fancy-dressed pirates and thrashed across the harbour, to a red and white buoy and back. In a fit of over-exuberant celebration, the pirates board their vessel while the trailer is still attached to the Insignia. The extra weight lifts the car's front wheels off the ground before the towbar pings clean off the car and everything crashes back to earth. Driver and pirates sit paralysed, stunned, until a cheer goes up from the hordes queuing for a pasty on the quayside and order is restored. The Vauxhall limps back up the road and the pirates paddle to the start line.

There's a man with a megaphone, but his enthusiastic instructions are drowned out by the crowds thronging around the pasty shop, the pub or the shack along the harbour wall that sells lobster rolls and local beer. This is the British foodie ideal writ large. No more will I lament that all our best seafood goes straight to Spain or Asia, nor that we're unwilling to pay for what's good. Here, the best of what's landed is eaten.

Or so it seems. Yesterday, newly arrived in Cornwall and rounding up some provisions along the coast in Newlyn for the next few days, I discovered, much to my delight, that the fish market is thriving. My wife is joining me for this leg of the trip, and a nice bit of locally caught fish should be just the ticket for our first night, I reasoned. This is a lively-looking town, and at first pass the shops behind the market are as readily frequented as any bakery anywhere in the country. There is a buzz and often a queue at each counter, and that's from all comers – not just the hoi-polloi who might be holidaying nearby. I step into each of them, my hands clasped behind my back and neck craned, trying to signal that I'm someone looking for something specific. It appears that the shopkeepers are too busy serving real customers to come and chat to me, so I head back out and prepare to take in the shops properly.

'Help you, squire?' I'm asked as I step into the fishmonger I'd previously singled out as looking particularly good, with a large, ice-filled display and a great array of shiny-looking fish.

'I noticed your scallop shells.'

'Three for five,' he nods at me, seeming to mark me down as a time-waster.

There's a chap fidgeting behind me in a waxed coat and leather wellingtons, his outfit suggesting that he's willing and able to splurge on a whim. The fact is not lost on the fishmonger, but not wanting to miss my moment, I press on.

'I just wondered if the scallops were local,' I say, scanning the icy trough in which the fish are displayed.

'She lives local, the woman that cleans 'em up … Can I help you, sir?' And with that I'm passed over.

'Eight tuna steaks … ' I hear over my shoulder as I step on to the pavement.

I wait a few minutes outside the shop, watching the crew of a day boat tidy away their tackle and other equipment while keeping an ear on the interaction carrying on in the fishmonger's. The well-dressed chap has bought a good amount of bits and pieces – pâtés and brown shrimp and rollmops – while also picking up some nice large prawns from the freezer section and a side of smoked salmon. Once I hear the slap of his leather wellingtons pass by, and the hearty thrum of a Mercedes estate start up, I pop back into the shop.

'Help you, squire?' He hasn't clocked me as a returning nuisance.

'What's good today?'

'Nice megrim in today. Plaice and pollock, too. Tail of a monkfish, there. Mackerel of course. How many you for?'

'My wife and I. Any tuna landed?'

'Fella avore took the last of it. We do get 'em landed, though they were bought in. Plenty of frozen bellytember there if something else takes your fancy.'

He's lost me slightly, but a gesticulation towards the freezer helps me understand what he means.

'And is the frozen fish landed locally?'

'I wouldn't say as much. Big prawns there from Thailand, far as I know. Squids too.'

'Much demand for local fish around here?'

'People want what people want.'

With that, I purchase a pair of megrim sole, lean, deep-water flatfish with a mild flavour and a flaky texture similar to plaice, and a couple of mackerel. It's good-looking fish of course, and both local and sustainable. As I sit in the car, plotting the route to my next stop, I can't help but wish the fishmonger had said as much. Or maybe he could have given me a knowing nod, perhaps shared a teasing exchange about how the fella before had missed the good local stuff and taken away a load of imported fish. We might have passed a few good minutes this way, him educating as I noted everything down. It didn't play out that way, of course it didn't – who am I to expect him to be a gatekeeper of British fish stocks, educator of the masses?

Back in the harbour at Porthleven, back in the present day, and with coffee secured, I head out to watch the raft race from the end of the harbour wall, a vantage from where I can also take in the town itself. The southerly most port in Britain, this little place of 3,000 residents hosts a food festival each year that draws at least that number again, and is home to some of the best surfing in Cornwall. It used to have a Rick Stein restaurant, and then a Michael Caines restaurant opened on the same site; both have since perished due to 'economic forces'.

This is not the most picture-perfect of Cornish towns. Porthleven has a workaday feel, and that is why it fascinates. The trendy coffee shop and its shiny roastery on the road into the town give the place a sheen, but otherwise there are a couple of pubs, a good few cafés and two or three busy pasty shops. There is a supermarket too, Pengelley's of Porthleven, which has a focus on Cornish goods and is housed in a warehouse close to the harbour. There are good Cornish staples here, saffron buns and Rodda's clotted cream and plenty of local veg alongside beers with pirate ships or the black and white Cornish flag. And there is meat branded as being from a local farm.

Pengelley's is charming, no doubt, but one can't help notice that many of the customers here today hold armfuls of cold drinks, packeted sandwiches, bags of sweets and the occasional pack of scones and cream – more the fodder of the holidaymaker than of the local. Although that alone is not to remove the significance from people's choices. What we eat at home on a midweek evening is very interesting to me, of course – it's what we've been recording thus far – but what we choose as holidaying Brits holds another layer of intrigue altogether.

In view of the former category, it must be noted that the heaving Lidl we stopped at on the outskirts of Helston that morning was much more indicative of the state of the British shopper looking towards a home-cooked meal. But to acknowledge that, like it or not, we're a nation that's fond of a packaged sandwich, sweets and regional afternoon tea fodder is not to diminish us as a food-loving nation. We've given packaged sandwiches to the world via Marks & Spencer, and as confectioners we have plenty to be proud of too. But even here, in Porthleven, a Cornish fishing village with some of the world's best seafood available within a minute's walk – and with the traditional pasty or the adopted banh mi, mac and cheese or Sri Lankan crab curry all available from market stalls lining the sea wall – we still queue for cellophane-wrapped scones and currant buns to be toasted and slathered in cream and jam for a mealtime that doesn't exist anywhere else in the world.

I will return to both afternoon tea and Lidl later, but for now I want to stay with Porthleven, a place indicative of two things. The first is the importance of coffee to the British diet. And the second is the place that pasties hold in the diet not just of the Cornish but of your broader Brit too.

As someone who grew up a long way from Cornwall, my main knowledge of the humble pasty has been either through its place in the Ginsters canon, often plucked from a fridge on long drives from London to Edinburgh as a student, or occasionally through the purchase of a treat from a West Cornwall Pasty Company kiosk in a train station. And the wonderful thing about pasties is that while these offerings are often mediocre when tasted alongside authentic examples, they're still a very workable gateway into the real deal.

Pasties have been a symbolic food of Cornwall and the south-west for over 200 years, although according to Hettie Merrick in her wonderful *The Pasty Book*, its roots are much older. The earliest mention of the pasty came in 1300, and it may be mentioned in Chaucer's *Canterbury Tales*. *The Pasty Book* also notes that in 1537, Jane Seymour was sent 'three pasties of the red deer' – at first glance a simple act of courtly gift-giving, but also a fascinating glimpse into the significance of the pasty in Tudor England. By the early sixteenth century, the once humble pasty was not merely a rustic meal, but a delicacy for the highest tables. To present a queen with venison enclosed in pastry spoke of abundance, generosity, and a nod to the careful stewardship of hunting rights, which were bound tightly to power.

For Cornish food culture, this moment underscores how the pasty existed simultaneously in two worlds: on the one hand, the practical fare of miners and labourers, designed to be eaten by hand; on the other, a luxurious courtly dish filled with prized game and elaborately spiced.

Properly defined as a turnover filled with either meat and potato or fruit, the reality is that the pasty probably wasn't invented in Cornwall. Early food-writing in Cumberland, Yorkshire, Lancashire and Lincolnshire refers to 'pies made without a dish, with the pastry rolled around the fruit or meat'. But the pasty became immortally Cornish in the eighteenth and nineteenth centuries, when many families in the county lived on or below the poverty line. At the time, pasties were a portable food that amounted to a complete meal, which could be made for little money. Apart from the flour, and perhaps a lick of beef, everything needed for a pasty could be brought together from what could be grown in a back garden. Hettie quotes travellers to Cornwall in the eighteenth century noting, 'both children and adults looked reasonably well nourished on what they [the travellers] considered a very poor diet'. Thank God for the pasty.

As was the case with so many of Britain's traditional foods, it was developments during the Industrial Revolution that helped put Cornish pasties firmly in the local – and then national – conscience. Holman Brothers Ltd was a mining equipment manufacturer founded in 1801, based in Camborne and Cornwall's largest manufacturer of industrial equipment. At its height, Holman's was spread over three sites and employed some three and a half thousand people. Alongside its industrial equipment for the mining industry, the firm also produced one of the very first solid fuel stoves for domestic use, better known nowadays as a range cooker. These appliances were not cheap, but before long everyone who could afford it had installed one in their home. For the first time, home cooks had control over their heat for baking that they hadn't had with the range's predecessor, the earthenware oven. The range meant a cook could control the temperature of their oven, and for the pasty in Cornwall this meant that the little parcel could be baked for a longer, slower cook, making the pastry flaky and delicious. And for those who couldn't stretch to having a range installed at home, they could take trays of pasties to their local bakery to be cooked in their commercial ranges once the day's bread was baked. I have marvelled at the romance of communities in Greece, Italy, Spain and Morocco who still make use of the local baker's oven for their own baking or for slow-cooking of pots of stew, which we in Britain were doing ourselves as late as the turn of the twentieth century.

In the popular telling, pasties became Cornish as a result of miners taking them to work for lunch, holding them by the thickest part of the crust so as not to cover the pasty in soot. There are also tales of mine owners providing ovens at ground level for miners to keep their pasties hot while they headed into the bowels of the earth to dig for tin and coal. What is less commonly known, however, is that at the end of the nineteenth century the price of tin plummeted, forcing Cornish miners abroad. They took pasties with them when they emigrated, which means that the humble pasty is now visible in the meat-filled pastries eaten in Mexico, South Africa, Canada, South America, the Caribbean and Australia. Whether it's a patty or an empanada, hand pie or manoletes, we can likely thank a Cornish miner for making the introduction.

We are not here to look backwards, but what I've learned so far in Cornwall is that the pasty is very much of the present day – and the future, too. Yes, we're a nation of magpies, but we're also good at knowing a good thing, and the pasty is certainly that. It helps, of course, that the Cornish can be bloody-mindedly independent. I keep reading how Cornwall is connected to the rest of the UK by a fine filigree 'thread on its Northern coast and by Brunel's great iron bridge over the Tamar in the south', which doesn't quite correlate to the geography of the UK as I am aware of it, and perhaps hints at a staunch Cornish few for whom even to travel to the county's northern border is to risk being hoovered up by the rest of England and thus become consumed by the beast. At any rate, mysterious Cornish geography aside, the pride of this place might have something to do with the continued popularity of the pasty here and across the country. Be it at Aunty May's in Newlyn, at Pip's Pasty Shop in Falmouth, at Porthgwarra Cove Café, or even at one of the chain of Cornish Bakery shops, you'll find meat and veg, cheese and veg or cheese and onion pasties that have been baked fresh that morning and are guaranteed to sell out before the day is done. Much as the locals hate to admit it, this is a tourist destination, so a little of this display of Cornishness is for show, but that is not to diminish its integrity.

So pasties are legit, but so too is our obsession with coffee, foreign pâtisserie, good bread, beer and cheese. And in Cornwall each of these is in evidence.

We started in the queue at Origin Coffee in Porthleven, and to that queue we'll now return.

Founded in 2004 by Tom Sobey, Origin is one of

Europe's leading speciality coffee roasters. They have a lovely but convoluted way of explaining what they do, but safe to say it involves paying fairly for the best coffee they can find, working to improve practices in the places they buy coffee from, and generally being good buyers, partners, consumers and custodians of the beans that are central to their existence. And their coffee is good, which is why the queue is so long. It's why hundreds of coffee shops across the country use their beans. And it's why this little corner of England is home to many of the best cafés I've stepped foot in, from Yallah in St Ives and Stones in Falmouth to Flora at Trelowarren and many more. The baked goods, bread, food and ambience of these places is so good that if you stumbled on it abroad you'd be basing next year's holiday around it and pitching it to Condé Nast Traveller to be on a list of *The World's Greatest Unknown Coffee Shops*.

In each of these places, and many more besides, you will find bread that's up there with the finest in the world. It is easy to poke fun at the sourdough movement that has spread across the UK and North America like wildfire. Sliced white, bloomer and cottage loaves can no longer hold a candle to the dusty mahogany crust of a perfect sourdough loaf. And where there is good coffee and good bread, there are also good baked goods. Much like the cornetti in Italy or the custard-filled pastries popular in Greece, the croissant is now as British as the all-day breakfast. Away from the trendy coffee shops of the type that I've mentioned, people frequent

Lidl and Aldi like the French use their local boulangerie. The morning queue at the bakery shelves in an Aldi near to where I live is not dissimilar to the queue at the pilgrimage-worthy Du Pain et des Idées in Paris, the home of the best croissant I've ever tasted. I heard one woman quip in the Lidl in Truro that she wouldn't be surprised if the chap behind the shelves wearing red oven mitts wasn't a top pâtissier flown in from France, so bronzed was each batch of croissants he nonchalantly tumbled down on to the shelf.

And yes, it's true that we have a proud lineage of fried breakfasts with toast to fill us up in the morning – and whenever I can get that kind of thing I embrace it wholeheartedly. If I spot kippers on a menu, that's breakfast sorted. Half a grapefruit, ideally prepared the night before, perhaps a sprinkle of caster sugar over the cut side like my grandparents used to do. Kedgeree, farls, porridge, hot soda bread and cold butter ... I could go on. These breakfast choices exist in people's memories more than they do in people's homes. I grew up in the 1980s and 1990s and our obsession with America, its television, its fashion and its foods ruined British breakfasts. We took some of the sugar out of course, but not all of it. Yet the 1990s boom in cereals in Britain was legendary; be it Cheerios, Cinnamon Grahams, Nesquik cereal, Golden Nuggets or Cookie Crunch, we welcomed the American influence with open arms. Add to that Ready Brek for sped-up porridge and Pop Tarts for a treat that combined jam on toast with a fruit pie, and the idea of spurtling a pan of rolled oats with a pinch of salt lost something of its allure. Anyway, into this slightly confused period of British breakfasting popped the croissant. Long thought of as French, the buttery crescent is actually a Viennese kipferl, an enriched yeasted roll popular in Austria since the thirteenth century. It is said to have migrated to France with Marie Antoinette, homesick as she was for the Viennese treats of her childhood; there is little proof of this, and it isn't until the mid-1800s that records show an Austrian, August Zang, opening a Viennese bakery in Paris. From there, the ascent of the croissant still took nearly seventy-five years, until in 1915 a chap called Sylvain Claudius Goy recorded the first-known French version of the croissant recipe using a laminated yeast dough instead of the brioche dough of the kipferl. To cut a long story short, the croissant arrived in Britain later than you might have expected, but its ascent was meteoric; it continues apace around the world, and nowhere more than in the UK. One can add a list of flaky, buttery and sweet pastries to our litany of adopted treats, but I can't help but feel our embedded fondness for pasties, pies and sausage rolls helped pave the way.

I leave Porthleven and head down the Lizard peninsula, crossing the windswept moors and careering down a single-lane road to reach Britain's most southerly café, Polpeor. Every time I've been to this place, whether it's spring, summer, autumn or winter, the café has been bathed in sunlight. It's a beautiful spot to sit on the terrace and eat something delicious while spotting seals on the rocks below. Unfortunately, on this visit I learn that the family who have run the café for the last three decades have decided to leave and hand the lease back to the National Trust – sad news indeed. Not because the offering was radically brilliant, but because it was a nice family-run place that did simple British dishes with a no-nonsense attitude and a smile.

This news digested, I order a fisherman's platter in place of the usual crab sandwich I tend to have here, which makes me very happy indeed. It brings together local prawns, picked white and brown crab meat, sweet little grilled sardines, a nice big mackerel, a bit of salad with a sharp vinaigrette and some crusty white bread and plenty of salted butter. I watch a seal and its pup playing in the bay as I'm enjoying this plate of fishy goodness, and think that it doesn't get much better than this. I then buy a Mr Whippy with a flake from an ice cream van as I walk back up to the car park and congratulate myself on enhancing a perfect lunch at the coast even further.

As you'll know by now, my hypothesis is that we Brits are magpies for delicious food and love adopting (or more often than not, adapting) food from outside our British isles into our national cuisine. Tired tropes from chicken tikka masala to the poor old stir-fry might still be prevalent, but we also find Ottolenghi-inspired rice dishes or delicious laksa and phos on dinner tables up and down the land.

As humbling as it is to admit, so far on my travels my hypothesis has repeatedly been proven wrong. I've got a green ring binder with pages of research on each place I've visited, and on each page for a new place there's a Post-it note with info about the demographic mix for that place, as well as some data from the most recent census on its cultural makeup.

According to the 2021 census, 96.8 per cent of the population in Cornwall identified as White. People could also specify as Cornish, and 117,000 people in the UK did so, 80,000 of whom lived in the county. So as I've already discovered, it makes sense that there's a strong sense of place in the food that's popular here. What it does also indicate is something I've always suspected: that down here, diaspora communities do not really exist in big enough numbers to have much impact on the food and drink of the region, apart from what I might term 'the usual' Chinese and Indian restaurants that I've found everywhere. I don't feel entirely comfortable using that term, but I think you know what I mean. The UK has a long tradition of pragmatic restaurateurs, often from Hong Kong or the neighbouring Guangdong region in the case of British high-street Chinese restaurants, or Bangladesh in the case of British high-street Indian restaurants, who have opened locally popular, British-centric restaurants in villages up and down the country. I appreciate that this is not the case everywhere; in other places on this trip I've eaten food from regional communities drawn from far and wide. But in Cornwall, as suggested by the data above, there is little in the way of food from elsewhere.

I will get on with my point eventually, but first I want to chastise myself. As I travel and make notes, I notice that I naturally pay more attention to food from certain countries than others. Malaysian food, for instance, is deemed of greater interest to me than American food, Vietnamese food is more interesting than Polish food, Gujarat cooking more fascinating than Romanian. The reason I say this here is that of course there is food in Cornwall from elsewhere. One of the largest diaspora in Cornwall is from Poland, and in the larger centres, whether Newquay, Redruth or Truro, I've happily shopped in one Polski Sklep or another. Equally, American food, Italian food and Caribbean cooking are just as well presented in Cornwall as they are in many places around the UK, but I might have ignored them, thinking they were less deserving of analysis.

It is with these jumbled thoughts hurtling around my head that I cross Cornwall, hoping to prove or disprove my theory. And on the drive out to the Lizard, my interest is piqued by three places: an old-school Chinese restaurant inside a 1930s house that has been made to resemble something from the Tang Dynasty; a roadside shack housing what calls itself an authentic Thai restaurant; and a Mexican restaurant shoehorned into what was once a typical British caff. Retracing my steps after lunch at Polpeor, I ruled out the first two places having parked up the car and taken in the Thai restaurant's thirty-odd-page menu, and something that resembled an R&D meeting of a microwave ready-meal brand at the Mexican spot. Perhaps I should have ventured inside in the name of research and given both places a chance, but I go with my gut and conclude that neither place is going to deliver much of an insight as to what people in Cornwall typically eat. After all, both places are completely empty on a Saturday lunchtime.

Unbowed, I press on. A quick Google search on my phone brings up the menu for Dynasty just outside Penzance, the Chinese restaurant inside the 1930s house, and initial signs are good. A declaration at the top of the menu that 'We use fresh local produce where possible' gives me hope. And names of certain dishes suggest a place that's trying to do more than just trot out tried and tested British-Chinese culinary tropes.

Pulling into the car park, the bit of me that pressed eject at the previous two restaurants flares up again, but I'm keen to follow through on my hunch. I spend my life heading into dimly lit dining rooms hoping that what comes out of the kitchen is going to change me for ever. I'm proven wrong infinitely more times than I'm proven right, but it's the knowledge that I can be right that drives me on.

And so it was that I found myself walking along the bright red corridor that leads from the pagoda entrance to the red, gold and marble bar. I placed a takeaway order and waited opposite a large fish tank, while something in me started to twitch. A low hissing hum was coming from a room out of sight. I could also hear the shuffling of cardboard and the occasional crash of spoon against metal tray. I followed my ears until I was standing in what, on busy nights, would be the main dining room, staring at a buffet set-up from which my order was being fulfilled. I love a Chinese buffet as much as the next irony-embracing foodie, but I mention it because what I was witnessing made it all too clear that my order of crab claws was not going to be authentic, delicious and caught that day, and nor were my spring onion and ginger prawns going to be fat, shell-on treats.

Returning to the car, it was hard not to feel forlorn. That said, the part of my brain that wants to find authentic Chinese food in remote parts of the UK is not necessarily logical. Anything sickly and saccharine does nothing for me. I was charmed by the chicken wings I ate in Scotland, but that was partly because one place had a singular obsession with them. But when every roadside pub in Cornwall serves pulled pork or mac and cheese with candied jalapeños, I'm not whooping and wanting to fill this book with odes to hot sauce or orange cheese. And yet if the sheer volume of menu listings was the deciding factor, the new British menu in Cornwall would certainly include all those things.

*

The South-West

And so it is that I return to Porthleven, the morning after the night before. I want to stock up on Origin coffee beans and decide to pick up a few pasties for the road. So after a stop at the plush Origin warehouse I park in the centre of Porthleven and walk towards the café on the seafront that was most popular when I was last here. Today, though, I notice an alleyway that cuts behind the town and leads to some food businesses I didn't spot previously, no doubt because I was distracted by the pirate race. And so, in what turns out to be a courtyard of light industrial units, there is a bagel shop, a bao-buns-meets-laksa place, a brewery and a juice bar. And suddenly I have a sense of what Cornwall's version of a new British menu might just look like. We have links to the sea that are evident in crab sandwiches, fish and chips, seafood platters and fishcakes, and we have a magpie selection of foods from around the world that have been adopted not because of their links to the Cornish population, but because of their suitability to the typical lifestyle of your modern Cornwall dweller. The food is therefore influenced as much by California or Bali as it is by London – and there's nothing wrong with that. Perhaps if Cornwall has taught me anything, it is that immigration is one factor that can affect the food we adopt as ours, but social media and the global trends it pushes on us is another.

And with that revelation ringing about my head, the time has come to head up the motorway towards

London, and the final two stops on this voyage of discovery. On the way, though, a reward for a voyage almost completed.

I'm still trying to process what I experienced at Coombeshead Farm, the collection of dairy farm buildings within spitting distance of the A30 at Launceston, just inside the Cornish border, that opened in 2016 as a guesthouse with an on-site restaurant, bakery and working farm. It's a living, breathing vision of what the future of food and farming could look like. There's something incredibly grounding about standing on a sixty-six-acre site where every square foot feels cared for and respected – and from where almost everything you eat is farmed.

What struck me most was the long-term mindset. As any farmer might say, the aim is to leave the land better than they found it – but here they're actually doing it. Replanting, restoring and replenishing is at the heart of the philosophy. The farm itself is a beautiful mosaic of meadows, pastures and woodland. It vibrates with life – not just of animals, but a diversity of species that evidently thrive in this environment. When I first read about Coombeshead, it was on the back of Tom Adams's success with Pitt Cue, a pork-based BBQ spot in London that went from airstream trailer to trendy restaurant – and then to swanky behemoth. Pitt Cue burned bright for a while, but Tom had a dream to breed Mangalitsa pigs, so retreated to Cornwall and did just that. I got to see and eat the pigs, and the beef and lamb too, but what really stayed with me was how at Coombeshead they're listening to the land, to the changing needs of the ecosystem, and to their own instincts. They've shifted from being pig-centric to being place-centric. Which takes vision, and might just show a way forward.

The control they have over everything at Coombeshead, from soil to shop, with the restaurant and one of Britain's best bakeries, is rare and powerful. You can taste the difference in everything there. But more than that, you can feel it. There's something quietly radical about Coombeshead. It's not shouting for attention. It's just doing the work, beautifully.

Is it possible for the whole of Britain to adopt the Coombeshead way? Well, of course, but it would take radical change. That said, from what I've seen in Cornwall, things like pasties have survived in a way that traditional foods haven't elsewhere, thanks to local pride. There's an emphasis on doing things properly, whether in Origin or in Polpeor café, and now at Coombeshead, too. More and more places up and down the country are aligning with how Tom does things, and so perhaps British food in the near future could be about a new way of producing the food we eat, as opposed to how I tend to expect the future of British food to unfold – as a conveyor belt of soon-to-be-adopted dishes, old trusties, new ways with old dishes and dishes from elsewhere that we haven't even had a peek at yet, that may reflect Britain as it is now and in the future. I suppose what Tom, and others like him, have made me see is that it might be the farmers and producers that make food in new, sustainable and more delicious ways who end up suggesting more about the future of British food than just identifying a new list of dishes that we all enjoy. Which I suppose is how it once was – and still is in countries that remain aligned with their agrarian roots. I'm thinking about Spain, Italy and France – and many more besides.

8

The South-East

Home territory, that's what we now approach. For disclosure's sake, this is my turf. A lily southerner, whose record on Ancestry.com will show barely a soul from my lineage who has made their home further north than Suffolk or further east than Wiltshire. My grandfather was born in Stoke Newington, a cockney born within the sound of Bow Bells, both grandmothers born in the suburbs of south-east London, both parents born and raised in Surrey. My maternal grandfather grew up in India, to parents from England, but attended boarding school in the south-east and never returned to live there; thus a modicum of interest is snuffed out and an entirely commuter-belt lineage can be pieced together.

Despite travelling up from the south-west, I decide to navigate around London and start this leg of the journey in Colchester. It lays claim to being the oldest town in England and would become the Roman empire's first major outpost in Britain and thus our first capital city, known as Camulodunum. Charming as Colchester is, today I'm passing through in order to get to Mersea

Island, where the Company Shed has been trading since 1985. Once a purification plant for oysters, this black shed is now one of our greatest seafood restaurants – not that you'd know to look at it. I first came out here in 2010 with a few chefs who liked to spend their midweek days off picking up a baguette and a bottle of wine before driving east to sit and eat some of the best and sweetest oysters and shellfish you'll ever find. The tide is a tinker out here, and without checking the times in advance you can easily get cut off, so the whole caper always felt exotic and exciting. There was a rumour that the Company Shed had closed, but thankfully she's open for business and thriving and so I'm on my way.

When it comes to food, most of England's southeast is in the shadow cast by London, and you might expect the food culture to be a pale imitation of what's on offer in the capital. But the reverse is true, at least in this corner of Essex, which is remarkable for its productivity. As I motor along, I see signs to Tiptree and Maldon and make a mental note to take a detour on my way back towards Colchester after lunch.

Having parked a short walk away, I approach the Company Shed hoping I might have caught it on a quiet lunchtime, so I can get a seat and take my time, observe and perhaps ask a few questions. The approach to the restaurant is always pleasing. The Company Shed consists of a series of black, timber-clad sheds, and it is surrounded on either side by moored sailing dinghies. Beyond that there is the Blackwater Estuary, which has more boats on it – and so as you approach, you hear the pinging and clattering of rigging as the wind whistles around the masts. The noise might be annoying for locals, but for the visitor heading to the sheds, it is a siren call, a beckoning, for great seafood lies where the peal of the rigging meets the water.

There is no wind to speak of today, so my approach is silent, though the place is heaving and I queue a little to get in. Inside there are long tables, one with a local family celebrating a birthday, and next to them a Turkish family, a pile of delicious-looking flatbreads, and a carrier bag of long green peppers open on the table. Otherwise, dotted around the room are mothers with pushchairs and kids doing drawings at the table, a table or two like myself, out from London to worship at the altar of fresh seafood, and a couple of regulars who seem to know the owners.

At one end of the room there are trays and tanks filled with oysters as well as crabs, cockles and winkles, and cordoned off from the dining tables by shower curtains depicting a cartoon aquarium – an on-the-nose choice, but the interiors are not why I'm here. To my left as I enter is a counter piled high with fresh fish and some other bits and pieces that I hope to soon enjoy as part of a whole crab platter. I've rung ahead to pre-order that, so I fancy my chances of having a wonderful time. It is nirvana here.

Later, I'm stuffed, with sticky fingers and with the sweet detritus of shellfish splattered all down my shirt.

I've also enjoyed the mineral succour of twelve local oysters, ordered in two batches of six so good were they, so plump and sweet yet with hints of pickled cucumber as a background note behind the briny wash. I walk to the water's edge and, uncharacteristically, decide to take a quick dip. I'm not the only person swimming, but it's certainly not a communal activity here. Anyway, wading in I notice the muddy silt of the seabed and as I wallow in the unseasonally warm water I wonder why this little spot is so good for oysters. One of the ladies working in the shed told me they still hand-rake the oyster beds and harvest everything using traditional methods. And oysters have thrived in these waters since Roman times. It is a common boast here, and in Whitstable, that oysters were shipped from here not just up to Colchester but to Rome itself, so legendary was their quality. Given the lack of refrigeration in those days, and the length of journey, I've always assumed this boast to be apocryphal, but I like it all the same.

The water in this part of Essex is brackish – half salty seawater and half mineral-rich freshwater from inland rivers – which is just the thing for growing delicious oysters. And the silty mud combined with the shallow waters helps keep the temperature warm, coupled with the tides that refresh the water constantly. This explains why the oysters I had today were so exemplary. And so, once again, I've noticed a thing we're good at, that is cherished and eaten locally, and whose appeal draws people from all over to come and enjoy it too.

The South-East

Back in the car, soggy, sated and smug, I take the chance to make a few quick notes. 'We don't always have to just adopt and adapt other people's food – we've got enough good stuff to make more of.' And then, 'Sometimes our own food is good enough for everyone, and not old-fashioned at all. Just as good now as it was then, and good for the future too.'

Then, on the road, I drive past the gates of the Tiptree jam factory, my nose detecting the scent of lemon curd and boiling raspberries – or so I convince myself. And then there are signs for Maldon, where I once stayed on a boat that, long ago, was used to harvest the famous salt. I once heard that if all the salt sold as being from Maldon was actually harvested there, you'd be able to walk from the harbour to the Hook of Holland. I decide not to visit today, but I'm sure that isn't true – I don't wish to cast aspersions on the good people of Maldon Salt. Like Mersea, Maldon lies on the Blackwater Estuary, and just as the oysters downstream benefit from the river's salinity and minerals, this is a perfect spot for harvesting good salt. There are Roman salt baths in Maldon, not for bathing but for salt extraction – Romans would have used clay-lined evaporation ponds and boiled brine in lead pans to extract the salt from the seawater. In fact, the salt producers here were recorded in the Doomsday Book. They still make the salt using the same techniques, but in a proper factory. The process involves taking seawater from the estuary and evaporating it; the result is the pyramid-shaped flakes Maldon salt is renowned for, a result of hand-raking the crystals from the pans, then drying them further. We should be proud of Maldon for giving us proper, completely natural salt – from a family-owned company, no less. It's a properly British ingredient that's recognised the world over. Hooray for Maldon.

I park up in Chelmsford, just a few miles upriver, keen to get a fresh perspective on Essex from a commuter town that I gather is on the up. And barely a minute after walking towards the town centre I can see why. The high street has all the normal bits and pieces – shoe shops, clothes shops, a W H Smith – but there's also a throng of hungry people queuing up around a series of stalls, food vans, artisan bakers, fish and cheesemongers, a mix of local specialities and vendors from further afield.

I am stuffed, my Sisyphean curse on this journey, yet the smells emanating from a Caribbean food truck are particularly hard to ignore – and neither is the queue snaking down the street. I ask a woman who has just got her food what she recommends, and she opens her box to reveal a dark and unctuous goat curry that smells delicious.

'They're just sold out,' she tells me, her face a picture of sympathy, 'but Caribbean Flavour is worth a try, or Pamz. Or get the oxtail? Or the brown chicken. And the mutton is good, too.'

'Where else should I try?' I ask, judging this woman to have good taste.

'Jerk Station,' she says, quick as a flash. 'Good Jerk there, obviously, but the ewa too, and the jollof. Or the fried snapper, rice and peas. You can't go wrong.'

I thank her and walk away, cursing my greed at the Company Shed – before consulting my map and plotting a route via all of them anyway. Each offers a sensory treat as I peer in and pass by. Jerk Station is near where I parked, so I reason I could treat myself to something for the road – that is until I pass an Afghan stall selling a slightly inexplicable mix of nuts, sweets and baklava, as well as samosas and some sort of stewed lamb served with saffron-flecked rice. I cave and order a portion of the lamb and a samosa. And again at Jerk Station – a patty, some ewa and a small portion of jerk wings. Back in the car, I tear into the various packages, allowing myself a taste of everything while saving space for what is to come. It is all sublime, the samosa expertly spiced, the lamb soft but with crispy sections of still-intact skin, and the creamy beans of the ewa, topped with a smoky pepper sauce, is a comfort I didn't know I needed. I knew I was right to trust the lady from the queue; I never would have ordered Nigerian beans in a jerk spot without her tip-off.

The experience makes me reflect. For every street food stall serving deliciousness on the high street in Chelmsford, there was a Breakfast Club, or a Côte or a Pizza Express or a fried chicken shop. And for every customer at the stall selling local cheeses, a reflection of a thriving local industry, there are two or three at the

Breakfast Club. Both things can coexist in Chelmsford, but it's hard to understand why we're so much more likely to stick with chain restaurants without considering the possibility – and the deliciousness – of what else might be on offer. People like what they know, I suppose.

I am back on the road and heading south towards Southend to see what glamour the world's longest pier can add to a place.

Arriving in the town, I have the same feeling I had descending into Scarborough, or as a child visiting friends and relatives in Weymouth and Eastbourne: a pleasing childhood nostalgia for the seaside frippery of neon signage and pastel-coloured ice cream parlours, along with the hope of fried foods and sugary drinks. On the other hand, the seaside recalls the sadness of empty arcades and the whipping sound of cheap cagoules as clouds roll in and old women sit huddled in any shelter they can find, hoods up and tied about their jowls. It only takes twenty minutes or so for me to experience all the above, and by the time I'm paying six pounds to walk the 1.33 miles to the end of the world's longest pier I feel discombobulated.

Reaching the end of the pier, though, a new joyfulness has found its way into me. What a marvel this thing is. It has its own train, although I'd recommend the walk if you want to clear your head. By the time I reach the end I feel like I'm in the middle of the sea, although officially speaking I'm in the middle of the Thames Estuary. As I stand with land on my left, all I can see is the North Sea. Turning around, I see the land narrow at the horizon, and the scent of salinity that cleared my mind seconds before turns to engine oil and the slight whiff of an open drain as I stare back towards Gravesend, Dartford and the Thames Barrier in the distance. I want to ask someone if they can smell it too, but no one else is out here. Lightheaded, I fear that I might collapse, out here on my own, so take a seat and stare out at the Hook of Holland somewhere over the horizon. I take out my phone to check my bearings, and also to Google the symptoms of a stroke, only to see that ahead of me now is where I am headed, Sheerness, the Isle of Sheppey and Whitstable. If only I could carry on walking, save the drive.

Instead I sit a little longer and eat one of the patties I've been carrying with me since Chelmsford. Marvelling at its lightness and flavour, I feel grounded once again. Then I remind myself of the places here I'd singled out as being of interest. Unlike Scarborough, my last British seaside jaunt, Southend feels like a real place. Life is happening in tandem with the singsong of seaside holidays, so there are arcades and a German Doner Kebab franchise, there's an Odeon cinema and a rickety rollercoaster overlooking the beach, there's a Victorian lift by the cliffs as well as a shopping centre with a TK Maxx and a Poundland. Among all that there are a few old-school Italian ice cream parlours, some Italian restaurants, more well-liked Caribbean places and a couple of noted seafood shacks. A pattern is emerging for this corner of Essex: world-class seafood and excellent jerk, ice cream and curry goat.

As it is I stroll back towards land, relieved that I'm not having a stroke after all, and think about what I might eat next. I don't especially want to eat the same sort of meals I've had in West Mersea and Chelmsford – could anything in Southend beat them, anyway? So instead I opt for Rossi's, an ice cream parlour on the esplanade that's the pride of the locals. I take my place alongside the pensioners and parents with toddlers, and order an Arctic Coffee and a lemon ice, sorry that I don't have room for the cherry ice cream, the famous apple pie with award-winning vanilla ice cream, the banana split and the coke float. The lemon ice is the perfect antidote to my creeping claustrophobia. It is so sweet and so sharp that I'm transported back to Italy and the first ever lemon sorbet I had as a child, scooped out of a hollowed Amalfi lemon as large as my head. And who doesn't love black coffee with a scoop of vanilla ice cream – it's affogato by another name, but here they call it Arctic Coffee, which somehow seems very British.

I get back in the car and drive out to Osborne's, officially in Leigh-on-Sea, and on the way pass a handful of Turkish spots that look enticing. I find myself thinking of Sheesh, the bizarre 'Turkish' restaurant with branches in Chigwell and Piccadilly Circus, that was made famous by *The Only Way is Essex* and offers Wagyu Sheesh for £90 and cheesy chips for £26. It seems the success of Sheesh has spawned a series of imitators, or maybe I'm being unfair. Perhaps they're not imitations at all, and this is a legitimate stylistic choice for a modern British Turkish eatery. Being very familiar with the ocakbaşları that can be found around Green Lanes in north-west London, I've come to expect a limited decor, with the focus being the long grill, not to mention the puffs of smoke and sizzle of fire as fat from good meat drips on to the hot coals. I assume the place I've passed, Baboush, is similar to Sheesh; the decor is glossy black and gold, and the menu board outside includes pictures of cocktails with sparklers. At Sheesh, a portion of lamb chops is £68 and the kofte is £38; here, they are priced at a much more reasonable £22 and £16, but that still sends me into a spin. Turkish food should be delicious, smoky, riddled with herbs and molasses and lemony sumac sharpness, and if not cheap then at least affordable. But thinking again, I'm struck by my own snobbery. Why would I happily pay £30 plus for good meat and sides from a trendy restaurant with an Instagram-famous chef, but then expect my chicken sis and lamb chops to be a fraction of the price? Once I've stopped outside Osborne's I quickly look up the menu at Umut 2000, my most frequented Turkish ocakbaşı in London, and note that their lamb chops are £27.50 and their adana £19 – and quite right too. We all have a tendency to overvalue certain cuisines and undervalue others, but I was quietly

All You Can Eat

delighted that the large portions of curry goat and oxtail at Jerk Station were only £10 each.

Having made it over QE2 bridge at Thurrock and along the Kent coast to Deal, where I stay overnight, I wake the next morning to consider my options. I am keen to head north to Whitstable, partly to look back at Southend from this side of the estuary, and partly because I've become obsessed with finding the Dredgerman's Breakfast, a fabled dish apparently unique to Whitstable – and something I read about when researching this book.

'I'm looking to try a Dredgerman's Breakfast?' I say to the lady behind the counter at the Whitstable Oyster Company, my first port of call having arrived in town and one of Whitstable's most well-known seafood institutions, the anticipation making me feel like a spaniel at the prospect of a walk.

'Never heard of it,' comes the reply.

'It's an old-fashioned thing. Traditional here, I think. The old oyster fishermen used to eat it.'

'Really sorry,' she says, 'I'm genuinely not sure what that is. Try Wheelers?'

And so to the other extraordinary seafood spot in town: 'No idea. We have oysters though, and rolls.'

'Have you heard of it, though?'

'I'm really not sure that's a thing.'

'It's never been on the menu, not even in the beginning?'

'Nope, not here.'

Before long, I've tried every café, every restaurant, every butcher, fish shop and chippie in Whitstable; I've walked the high street from where I parked the car, following the crisp saline scent on the wind down to the harbour, and back again. I've been told that what I'm looking for is not a thing – and if it is, it certainly isn't from here. And even though I'm pretty sure it is a thing, even though I've read about it on Glyn Hughes's wonderful website, *The Foods of England Project*, I'm starting to doubt myself. The thing is, the Dredgerman's Breakfast sounds wonderful: a local bap known as a huffkin, stuffed with freshly shucked oysters and a few rashers of bacon, adorned with nothing else but a few grinds of black pepper and washed down with a salty local porter. What's not to love? But as I field rejection after rejection, I'm on the cusp of giving up.

If Britain's culinary future rests on striking a balance between reinvention and integration on the one hand, and recognising what's good about our traditions and preserving them on the other, I'm not seeing a lot of that in East Kent today. In fact, from the little I've seen so far, the opposite might be true.

On my drive from Essex to Whitstable, I've felt a growing unease that, lovely as it is out here, lots of people are desperate to be elsewhere. Or perhaps a better way of putting it is that people are desperate for this to be somewhere else. On the road from Canterbury to Whitstable, I saw a pub with a big banner that read 'Miami Pizza Co. available here now!' and a garden nursery offering to sell me potted herbs from a company named 'Malibu Herbs'.

And so, I've decided that the Dredgerman's Breakfast is the thing that will ground me here, give me the truest sense of what Kent is like when it's not trying to be somewhere else. And if I can find some traces of it, if I can locate its heartbeat in the current day, then surely I'll be off, a link from the past helping fire me into the future.

Much like the Company Shed and Osborne's, the Whitstable Oyster Company can trace its origins back to the 1400s – but Whitstable oysters go as far back as the Romans. Like Mersea and the River Blackwater, Whitstable's position at the mouth of the River Swale, with freshwater nutrients mixing with the salt in the Thames Estuary, gives it the same shallow, sun-warmed waters that are the perfect place for oysters to breed and grow. At the company's peak in the 1850s, it was sending as many as 80 million oysters a year to Billingsgate fish market, about half the total consumed each year in the capital – the plentiful mollusc had become the food of the beer-swilling poor.

It used to be that a large fleet of up to eighty smacks and yawls, fishing boats specifically finessed for the task of harvesting oysters, were moored off the beach to dredge the oyster beds. Sadly, according to the Whitstable Oyster Company, 'two World Wars, the great flood of 1953 and the introduction of the prawn cocktail', a cheap and cheerful seafood knickerbocker glory, saw the popularity of the oyster dwindle.

I'm walking these streets with all this maritime history sluicing about my head, but I'm getting blank looks and dismissive shrugs at every turn when I ask to taste a piece of it. It brings to mind a holiday in Corfu, when I dragged my long-suffering family up to a mountain village to eat lamb chops, despite the clear focus of most holidaying Brits, my family included, being proximity to the sea, tzatziki, grilled fish and ice-cold beer. Up in the hills, my espadrilles proved woefully inept among the weeds and thistles of the hillside tracks, but a salty wind occasionally offered momentary relief, and fatty smoke up ahead carried the scent of lamb. I passed crumbling building after crumbling building, beautiful grey stone buildings left to ruin, and then occasionally a breezeblock-and-concrete house, one or two storeys completed.

'Why does no one rescue these beautiful old buildings?' I asked my friend, a local.

'They're from when we were poor,' he explains. 'We can have new buildings now.'

We can have brand-new dishes now in Whitstable, too. The menu at Wheelers Oyster Bar, which I stare at while being told my hoped-for breakfast doesn't exist, promises seafood prepared with ingredients from across the globe: ceviche, curried crab, Szechuan pepper squid, jerk-spiced monkfish, lobster and 'nduja lasagna. I can have brand-new things now.

All You Can Eat

Dejected and at the end of town in the old commercial harbour, I try one last place, a shipping container with a chalkboard menu and some oysters on ice on the counter.

'I'm hoping to try a Dredgerman's Breakfast – I think it's bacon and oysters in a roll.'

I'm almost certain by now that the breakfast I'm after is a myth. It's certainly not a thing readily available here. Having said that, it's hardly a leap of faith to imagine some of the old seadogs putting two and two together. God knows the market-holders in Billingsgate have been putting away scallop and bacon buns every morning for long enough; one can hardly ignore the chance that the salts in Whitstable might have done the same with the oysters they were hauling up from the sea floor.

'Sorry, mate, never heard of it,' the dreaded-but-familiar refrain. 'You could order a bacon roll though, and the oysters were dropped off just now.'

And so I'm off. I order one bacon bap and a half-dozen fresh oysters. I'm yet to hear a single local confirm that a Dredgerman's Breakfast has ever existed, but I don't care. This is how it would have been.

Before long, a wooden tray with six shucked oysters nestled in ice is placed in front of me, along with a bacon roll. The bap is probably from a supermarket multipack rather than a local bakery, but I'm only a few deft moves away from a Dredgerman's Breakfast, and I'd happily make do with a couple of sheets of corrugated cardboard if it meant I could finally eat this thing and start my day of culinary discovery.

I open my bacon roll and lay a few oysters on top of my bacon. Visually it's not as appealing as the scallop and bacon combination that has endured at Billingsgate.

'Any sauces?' the nice man from the shipping container asks, placing a pepper grinder and a bottle of Tabasco on the table.

I have no idea of the right answer. My memory is that black pepper would have been traditional, but how can there be a tradition if no one thinks the thing exists?

'Brown?' I say, thinking about what I'd normally have on a bacon sandwich. But before the bottle of HP Sauce arrives on the table, I take a bite. And suddenly it is all worthwhile.

There is an alchemy, I've now discovered, when a cold, minerally oyster meets hot, smoky, fatty bacon, and it is transportive. I was taken back to hot childhood holidays on British beaches, to mouthfuls of seawater and burnt barbecue sausages on the beach. And to Portugal and grilled sardines with ice-cold but flavourless beer. It has a hint of brackish swill about it, but an unctuous smokiness, too.

'If someone did these out of a little hatch on the front, they'd sell like hotcakes,' I shout to the lads shucking oysters in the back of the shipping container, my excitement returning every time I take another greedy mouthful. They don't hear and I don't repeat myself.

I like the Dredgerman's Breakfast, though. I like it very much.

So much so, in fact, that I buy another half-dozen oysters to take away and plan to make a detour on the way home to an old bakery in Wingham that still produces proper old-school Kentish treats. I'll buy a round of huffkins, and will add a gypsy tart for good measure. You don't often find gypsy tarts outside of Kent, but they're a saccharine treat that combines demerara sugar and condensed milk in a flaky pastry case and is guaranteed to give you fillings if you eat more than one a year.

And so that is Whitstable, a charming place with all the trappings you'd expect of a nice town in the southeast of England. It has a high street that bends down to the seafront, with sourdough bakeries, gift shops, butchers and fruit and veg shops, and pubs with great local beers. On the seafront there are seafood restaurants and oyster huts and shacks selling snacks that will knock your socks off. It's not a sit-on-the-beach-after-a-bracing-dip sort of seafront, but the sort of place where you might grab a stout and a dozen oysters and enjoy them with your socks off and your jeans rolled up, with your feet in the icy shallows. And then, along the coast at Seasalter, there's a Michelin-starred pub called the Sportsman, where you order at the bar despite all its accolades, and where, if you're lucky enough to snare a table, you'll probably have one of the best meals of your life.

The South-East

The thing about Kent, and the rest of the south-east of England too, is that it is inescapably in thrall to London, and thus in its service. From a food perspective, that means that the farming and fruit growing there is largely for the restaurants of London, while its restaurants and dining scene are largely influenced by London – and the people who live here largely do so because of its proximity to the capital. I'm oversimplifying, of course, but it is the truth, and it means that more than anywhere else I've been on this trip, I feel London's shadow looming wherever I turn. Even out here on the east Kent coast, an hour and forty-five minutes by train from the capital, London is in the air.

Back in Deal the next morning before heading off, I visit the Black Pig for some bacon, a proper butcher who sources very good meat locally, my rashers of smoked back bacon having come from Snoad Farm in Faversham.

And then, ensconced in the kitchen on a grey day and in need of perking up before I continue my explorations, I fry the bacon, shuck yesterday's oysters and spread salted butter on the bottom half of a toasted huffkin, before layering spitting hot bacon and cold fresh oysters into the thing. Today, all that's needed is a bit of black pepper on the oysters.

Even at home, it is good. I'm not being lashed across the face as I eat by a wind that's equal parts diesel fuel and sea salt. I'm not in the harbour sitting on buckets and leaning on crates that contain ropes and buoys. I'm certainly not crunching about on shingle containing century-old oyster shells, ground into rough sand by the daily machinations of this busy harbour. I'm in my slippers at the kitchen table, plotting my route to Lewes and watching YouTube videos of Korean street food vendors. And yet, somehow, nothing of the magic of the Dredgerman is lost; if anything, the black pepper with the smoky bacon fat and salty oyster is an improvement on yesterday's HP Sauce and allows the sandwich to sing.

Where once the Dredgerman didn't exist, I've now had two in as many days – and with that I'm off across the south-east with three farms in my sights. The first will be Brogdale, outside Faversham, home of the National Fruit Collection, then I'm heading to East Sussex to visit Namayasai, a no-dig Japanese-style farm near Lewes. Finally, I'll be visiting the legendary Knepp Estate in West Sussex, where rewilding has replaced rows of cultivated crops and where from the wildness come wild plums, elderberries, grazing deer and pigs snuffling freely.

It's a strange business visiting a farm. Unlike when you sit down in a restaurant, snoop in shops or even ask others what they eat at home, there's little to taste. It's even stranger at the National Fruit Collection at Brogdale, where in collaboration with the University of Reading and DEFRA, 4,000 different varieties of fruit trees are grown, managed and harvested, making it a living 'gene bank' of the UK's cultivated fruits. At Brogdale, I walk through the orchards in bloom; there's no fruit on the branches, but there are thousands of varieties of apples and pears on their way. Only their names, pinned on signs staked in front of the trees, hint at the joy to come, each reading like a hopeful little poem: Cornish Gilliflower, Ashmead's Kernel, Norfolk Royal Russet. Kent has long been called the Garden of England, and here, among the blossom and buzz, you feel it – not as cliché, but as sensory truth. Down the road, there's a fruit farm that grows hardly anything but strawberries, almost all of which go to the Wimbledon tennis tournament each summer. The roads around here are punctuated every mile or so with roadside stands and stalls, often manned by a hardy soul sitting on a fold-out chair under an umbrella, or sometimes built up more like a garden shed with a makeshift counter, but always peddling the cherries, strawberries, apples and pears that make this rich little corner of England so worthy of its nickname at certain times of the year.

As I leave Kent and enter East Sussex, I'm reminded of my earlier suggestion that the south-east only exists in service to London, and wonder if I was being a little unfair. This network of roadside fruit stalls is bolstered also by a vast quantity of farm shops and delis, the quality of which you wouldn't believe. It has been a real disappointment in so many parts of the country, even parts with a rich history of producing food, that you can't turn off a main road near to almost every village and find a scrap of land with a shed or shack full of shelves of local produce, meat, fish, cheese and baked goods. I've visited more than a few on my travels around Britain, but in the south-east you find them at every turn – and for that the Home Counties can be proud. Although it's easy to be dismissive of commuters, with their big cars and suburban tastes, in reality there's a real appreciation for locally grown food down here.

At Namayasai Farm in East Sussex, just shy of the coast, they practise no-dig horticulture, a method of growing crops without ploughing the soil, instead relying on cover crops, mulching and natural soil ecology to maintain its fertility. Here they are cultivating daikon, shiso and mizuna with reverence and ecological rigour – and it's very impressive indeed. Namayasai has been in East Sussex since 2005, and they specialise in supplying high-end restaurants – inevitably in London. It reflects a wider desire to make the best of every cuisine without shipping authentic ingredients halfway around the world. We've adopted Japanese food into our British culinary arsenal as enthusiastically as any other cuisine. Be it sushi, sashimi, ramen, the high-street highlights of Wagamama or the high-end sushi tasting-menu restaurants, we are obsessed with Japanese food. And so Namayasai thrives. Has it had an impact locally? Absolutely – they supply boxes of their exemplary veg to lucky souls who live around Lewes, Seven Sisters and Haywards Heath, and I'm sure this will expand further in time. Because it is here, between Lewes and the sea, in a wealthy part of the country and only two hours from London, it has every chance. How shiso and mizuna might work their way into British daily cuisine is unclear, but edamame, wasabi, kabocha squash and yuzu already have, and the very delicious Japanese quinces or Balsam pears might find a home in our kitchens now that they're grown here. For what it's worth, I keep a bag of frozen edamame in my freezer for my toddler; as I've seen all over the UK, it's these kinds of small changes that form habits, that lead to the slow and steady acceptance of a new food into daily eating.

And with that in mind I complete my trip at the Knepp Estate, which in contrast to the low-key farming revolution at Namayasai has become world-famous for leading the way in regenerative agriculture. In 2001, the estate owners decided to stop farming the land around Knepp profitably, instead experimenting with allowing the ploughed land to become wild again, and seeing what this did for the birds, animals, insects and plants of the area – which survived and which thrived, and which new species arrived. They have a market garden at Knepp, as well as a shop and restaurant, and almost all the veg and meat is grown on site according to regenerative principles, or has been caught or foraged from the rewilded land. What does this mean for the menu? Well, Knepp beef and venison feature prominently, and so do quite a few vegetable dishes from the garden, particularly salad and greens. But then so too do all the usual suspects, things very much not from here, not from Knepp or even from these shores – halloumi, yoghurt, hummus, wild garlic pesto, rocket, Parmesan, lemons, blood oranges and the rest. This is not to cast doubt on the scheme, but to highlight how tough a project such as this is – and how much a certain strand of British food relies on ingredients that come from elsewhere entirely. Once upon a time, a British market garden would have yielded – depending on the season – peas, radishes, courgettes, asparagus, greens, salads, beans, potatoes, onions, wild garlic, samphire, salsify, sea kale, damsons, berries, plums, apples, pear, quinces, meats, fish, local cheeses and dozens more things to the menu. All this produce would have likely been included on a fairly traditional menu, with French, Italian, Spanish and some colonial influences cropping up here and there. So for a British rewilding project starting a market kitchen in the twenty-first century to feel obliged to buy in lemons, blood oranges, Parmesan, ricotta, halloumi, hummus and the rest shows how much these things have become part of the British menu. This is a market kitchen based on a radical rewilding project, and the fact that they lean on a list of non-native ingredients shows what consumers expect when they go out to eat. If Knepp want their kitchen to stay open, they have to serve food that people are willing to splash out on, so the cuisine is a British-Mediterranean mix, the recurring pattern of broad-brush

European cuisine with a dash of Middle Eastern food that most foodies would now consider unquestioningly British.

If this menu drew from the growing list of things from Namayasai Farm, a place where everything is home-grown, there would be some raised eyebrows. What's important for me as I head back home to the suburbs of London is that these new approaches to farming – and the menus that come out of their efforts – don't in any way reject tradition, whether deliberately or by accident. Instead, they are bringing traditions into the future, and that sense of possibility is what sticks with me as I get back in the car and head north.

As I join the A23 to cruise past Gatwick and into the sprawling suburbs of the capital, I'm trying to make shape of my time in the south-east; more than anywhere else I've been, it seems to be a region culinarily defined by its duality: does it look inwards, to its own traditions, or outwards, towards London and the world beyond? That tension is what gives the place its richness. On the one hand, there is extraordinary produce – oysters and salt from the Blackwater, fruit from Kentish orchards, meat from Sussex farms – that speaks strongly of place. On the other hand, there is the pull of London: its markets, restaurants and fashions drawing much of that bounty away, while giving back influences and expectations that filter down so that we have demand for the esoteric, the modern. To eat – and to exist – in the south-east is to live inside that push and pull, between the pride of tradition and the promise of novelty. The identity of the food culture here lies in its contradictions: a region that is both servant and rival to the capital, and one that reminds the rest of the country how good England's larder can be.

9

London

London is the best place to eat in the world. Much as I bore myself by writing something so trite, I fear that the phrase feels light for a place that simmers with so much good food, new food, and where its populace eats, seeks and cooks the new and the exciting with such ferocity that it seems to bend the country's taste to its will. London is not one of the world's great food cities because it tries to be – it is because the whole world seems to be here, cooking and eating.

And it never stays still. The city's food shifts with the tides: a new visa scheme, an overseas crisis, a viral Instagram post – each has an impact, eliciting change that ripples through neighbourhoods. Where other cities seem to fossilise their food traditions, London is a vortex, forever sucking in the flavours of elsewhere before spitting them back out as something new.

Perhaps it's the absence of an English food culture? Many would argue that in our markets and sandwich shops, our caffs and pie and mash shops, our butchers, fishmongers, greengrocers and pubs, we do have a definable English cuisine that still thrives in London, and in some corners of the city that is true. To what degree that exists purely for nostalgists and tourists is up for debate; I'd argue that the minuscule percentage of these businesses that retain their connection to the 1950s or 1930s are firmly propped up by misty-eyed purists (myself included) that want to keep them wrapped up in aspic for an occasional outing. For the rest of the time, London is changing year on year, month on month, week on week even, in thrall to the passing winds of globalisation and immigration. A change of immigration policy in Hong Kong will cause an influx of new expats to make their homes in London – and close behind them will be popular new additions to the London food landscape. A drop in the pound will see whole neighbourhoods suddenly bought up by the French, or Spanish, or by Emiratis or the wealthy from South America. And overnight, it seems, the most plugged-in corners of the internet will be raving about a new destination for food obsessives. Like any global city, the food culture in London is shifted by the cruelties of the world. Be it war, famine, terrorism, as soon as a new community arrives we'll see new flavours and styles of eating cropping up here and there. Before long, you'll notice morsels of that cuisine gracing high-street counters and corner-shop shelves; soon after it will appear at stalls in a market, then on restaurant menus. There can even be a feeling of whiplash when, within months of a humanitarian disaster, some influencer will go viral with the 'discovery' of a hidden gem, a new lunch option you *have* to try, an ingredient that will change your cooking *for ever*.

In the nineteenth century, London was often described as sucking in new arrivals and absorbing what they brought with them; Watson, in the first Sherlock Holmes novel *A Study in Scarlet*, referred to the city as 'that great cesspool into which all the loungers and idlers of Empire are irresistibly drained'. That's not quite how I would describe modern London, but the loss of traditional British cuisine has certainly left a vacuum into which the world's best foods get sucked. Londoners are open to new things, but it's survival of the fittest in a city vexed by rent increases and property speculation. A high street might be all ramen shops one year, only to be Syrian cafés and Uighur restaurants the next, followed by Korean chains, Georgian dumpling spots and the specific delights of West African cuisine. If I had written this book five years ago, ramen, hand-pulled Shian Xi-style noodles and Taiwanese bao would have featured heavily in London. As it is today, the best of these spots are still popular, but they're not as hyped as they once were. Instead, new dishes, new food cultures have arrived and caused a stir – and by next year the same will have happened again.

Few other cities have taken so many dishes from elsewhere so closely to their hearts. If the cuisines of our closest neighbours have been codified and set rigid, the recipes for 'proper' French or Spanish food fixed like a tapestry for all to admire, London is still out there like Fagin, considering what looks good and pick-pocketing indiscriminately. A Londoner doesn't take much persuasion to welcome shakshuka, babka, kimchi or injera into their diet.

So why the long preamble at the start of this chapter? Well … I am heading home, but I'm not going into London proper. I live in Kingston upon Thames, a London borough that is officially part of Greater London, but still regarded by those who have lived out this way longer than me as being part of Surrey. To my north are Twickenham, Richmond, Hounslow and Southall; to my east, New Malden and Tooting; my southern and western borders take me out of London entirely, so we can ignore those for now. The reason I sketch out my bordering neighbourhoods is that their names suggest one thing or another – posh West London suburbs on the one hand, scruffy borderlands on the other. Yet to someone with a greedy appetite for the best of London food, they suggest something else entirely. Hounslow and Southall (and Wembley beyond them) are the heartlands of some of London's finest South Asian food. Thriving Asian communities since the 1950s, the high streets are home to extraordinary South Asian clothes, jewellery, sweets, restaurants and more. London's best samosas? Southall. The best dosa? Southall. Jalebi? Southall. I could go on. Or you could go to Tooting, which has one of London's best indoor markets, and brilliant South Asian food all along the

London

main drag towards Tooting Bec that caters to every taste – from halal and vegetarian to buffet-style and BYOB – while over by the Common the streets are home to plenty of trendy restaurants. How can both these places be the home of London's best South Asian food? Easy. London is vast, and if you live near one of these places you'll understand the talent of the chefs and their vitality to the community. Step away from Leicester Square or any of the other major tourist traps, and you'll eat well, develop feelings for your patch and start eulogising about the food of that place, that market, that high street. You might find yourself saying that particular corner has the best food in London, and anyone who says otherwise just doesn't understand. But *you* know. And you'll claim it loudly and proudly, and then become very annoyed when people start to agree with you and travel across London to hype up your neighbourhood, which before long will become busier and more expensive. Eventually they'll leave and will start talking up another borough instead, with other food, from another community, and you'll go back to hyping your neighbourhood again, although it will have changed and absorbed other things. In the vortex, change is the only thing that is a constant.

In Twickenham, Chiswick and Kingston there exists a large Japanese diaspora that means fine sushi is available in much more relaxed settings than London sushi fanatics are used to. And the Turkish communities out here are as storied as those on Green Lanes and Dalston

Kingsland, in north-east London. That's not to say we don't have very traditional British food in south-west London. Kingston has one of England's oldest and longest-running outdoor food markets, its very existence set in law by royal charter. On the other hand, the town has welcomed the largest swathe of recent migration from Hong Kong. For those readers who aren't up to speed, in 2020, after China imposed a new national security law on Hong Kong, the UK government offered a special pathway to British National Overseas passport holders and their close family members. This new visa route allowed Hong Kongers to live, work and study in the UK, with the option to apply for permanent residency after five years and citizenship after six. It was presented as a response to the erosion of Hong Kong's freedoms, and the impact on the culinary future of Kingston has been nothing short of wonderful. What is fascinating about this most recent wave of migration to London is that it was led by a middle-class, educated section of society. So while much of migration is concerned with the movement of people at risk, or of people hoping to better their lot elsewhere, here this migration of an affluent slice of society in Hong Kong, moving to a salubrious part of London, has caused an excited influx of restaurants and shops to cater to this new audience – and it's happened fast. Some restaurant owners have literally packed up their place in Hong Kong and reassembled the same restaurant here, to serve the same customers. At some of my personal favourites, such as the spiced beef broth sellers by the Turk's Pier at Canbury Gardens, the spot on the one-way system whose name best translates as 'Fire Up the BBQ', and the Friday Night Market at the HKUK headquarters (a newly founded organisation for emigrants from Hong Kong), the marketing is done on Chinese social media, the menus are all in Cantonese; some of the payment processing options only work with Chinese accounts. It's all rather exciting. Some might spout bile about newly arrived migrants needing to assimilate, but these Hong Kongers grew up partly under British rule. Instead, there is carte blanche for these businesses to just do what they've always done. And they're not closed shops – the people of Kingston are warmly embraced into these new establishments, and we couldn't be more delighted for the new wave of culinary options.

The final piece in the puzzle of 'Why Kingston?' is the model of how London has always operated outside the commercial sector of its heaving centre. Areas like this were once called Metroland and known as places from where office workers commuted into Central London, but people gravitate to the outskirts to find space; as new communities roll through, how these outskirts look and operate flexes and stiffens to absorb or repel them, the passers-through, the government diktats and all the other bits and pieces that make a place's identity. While the West End becomes a playground for two or three massive property developers, places like Kingston, Romford, Croydon and Enfield are where London is most itself. I used to live in Kensal, Willesden and Harlesden; were I still there, this chapter would focus on those high streets, and the Irish, Portuguese, Brazilian, Somali, and other Latin American and East African diaspora communities that make those places such a joy to eat in. If I still lived in Finsbury Park, I'd be looking north to Wood Green and east to Tottenham, Stoke Newington and Dalston, unpicking how the Turkish, Kurdish, Syrian, Caribbean, South Asian and Eastern European communities have come together to create a new British cuisine for north-east London.

Here I am though, out in south-west London, exploring what British food in London looks like from here. Approaching from the south, I come off the M25 at Leatherhead and drive through Chessington (home to the eponymous World of Adventures). I am headed for New Malden – I want to start there, as it's the reason I was willing to consider moving to what is otherwise a fairly staid and suburban part of town. As I wend my way in on arterial roads that connect the big ring roads to the big smoke, I marvel at how New Malden came to be home to the largest Korean diaspora in Europe, but not in a way that they are siloed. There are over 120,000 Koreans residing in New Malden and its environs. Aside from restaurants and shops, there are Korean-language churches, schools, supermarkets and cultural centres. The train from New Malden to

London

Waterloo takes less than half an hour; this is a commuter town, and the high street also teems with the likes of McDonald's and Waitrose and Nando's and a Wetherspoons or two. There is a leisure centre and a B&Q. This is a typical London suburb, at once both very British and very Korean.

Most people are surprised to learn that New Malden has the largest Korean diaspora outside of Korea. And you can eat voraciously there, from all ends of the spectrum of Korean food – from the naughty, spicy, stringy cheese and fried treats to high-end Korean sushi, to Gogi-gu (or 'meat roast') restaurants, where the food is barbecued at a grill set in your table, or the finessed Korean finery of an extraordinary banchan – the side dishes, pickles and snacks served beforehand or alongside rice as part of a typical Korean meal.

My first stop is Chick and Beers – my favourite fried chicken restaurant in London, a short drive from my home in Kingston. As New Malden has been established as a thriving Korean diaspora since the 1970s, it is now in the stage of its development where second- and third-generation Koreans, who are both attached to their Korean heritage while also very much British, can unburden from their parents' consciousness of being migrants in this country, and are able to have fun.

As the name indicates, Chick and Beers serves only two things: fried chicken (with sides) and beer. For the most part, one orders a whole chicken, glazed or flavoured with sweet chilli, spicy sweet chilli, or garlic and soy. They butcher the chicken into fourteen or so pieces, bone in of course, the focus being maximum flavour here, then fry it; its brittle coating looks as if it has been dredged in cornflakes, so craggy is the batter. You can also get fries, Spam fritters and very cold beer. The unique Korean balance of spice, fermented funk and sweetness, combined with the propensity to put a shattering crispy thing with a soft slightly chewy thing, is hard to beat as a dining experience. My only advice is not to order Soju and start swirling it about in the bottle – leave that to the Korean hipsters.

For more traditional Korean dining, Imone is my favourite spot. Their banchan, a spread of cooked vegetables, pickled vegetables, stir-fries and fermented dishes, is laid on a tray for snacking and garnishing the rest of your meal; it is all made in house and is consistently the best I've had, such care and wizardry with seasoning do they possess here. Cake & Bingsoo is a fun café that makes, well, cake, while bingsu is the popular Korean dessert featuring a mountain of finely shaved ice, often made from frozen milk, topped with sweet additions like condensed milk, chopped fruit, sweet red beans and mochi (rice cakes). All of which means towering technicolour creations to sate a sweet tooth after a rich and spicy meal. Zazza is a Korean-Chinese spot hidden away through a door at the back of a convenience store; even without venturing much further than their signature jjajangmyeon (black bean noodles), a meal there is about the most delicious fun you can have just off an arterial roundabout anywhere in the world.

There are more good spots than bad ones in New Malden; if you venture down here, try anywhere that appeals to the mood you're in, and my bet is you'll leave satisfied. Oh, and don't refer to this as Korea Town or Little Korea; to my mind, that feels very American, and part of the subtle art of othering a place and a community so that it remains a spectacle to be gawped at. New Malden is just a London suburb where some of the tastiest food in the city can be found. Yes, much of it is Korean, sometimes very traditionally so, but more than that it is one style of food available on this high street. Whether you order fried chicken from Chick and Beers or from KFC, you're part of a London tradition for loving fried chicken – a very British peccadillo.

The reason for heading into London via New Malden, apart from some of Britain's best fried chicken, is that for my money, Korean-inspired foods have had the sharpest rise in popularity of any I have seen in recent history. As we saw in Lounges, every type of dining option, from chain restaurant menus to trendy independent spots, has, over time, accreted the joys of Korean flavours. Alongside Mexican influences, this has been the trend I've noticed most often. What makes this surprising, and hopeful, is that Korean flavours are not meek and mild; the unique petroleum-hum of the best kimchi or other fermented food is not for the faint of heart. And yet here we are, with kimchi and gochujang flavouring working its way into cheese toasties, burgers, mayonnaise, crisps and more. Maybe the groundwork was laid in our colonial past, where sambals and chutneys from around the world became piccalilli and the like back home. Either way, New Malden has been doing its thing since the 1970s; only now are we taking Korea's inimitable flavours to our hearts, but we're adopting them with gusto. The rest of the country follows where London goes, and where food is concerned the rise of Korean flavours bodes well for other cuisines that have for too long been at the sidelines of British culture.

Filled with beer and chicken, I make my way back to Kingston, passing the enormous H Mart, my go-to store for Korean and other Asian staples – as well as for the clingfilmed boxes of Korean sushi, or kimbap, my favourite being a minced beef and cheese treat that never fails to lift the spirits. I also pass Atariya Fine Foods, a Japanese wholesaler of some of London's finest sushi-grade seafood, and a place that serves some of the best-value sushi in the city.

I park at home and walk into the centre of Kingston. I'm heading to the market square, a place that used to host coronations – and no doubt beheadings. I'm no historian, but the market square is old – a couple of its buildings are genuinely Tudor, a few others Tudorbethan, the mock style of early twentieth century, yet it remains home to an array of fruit and veg stalls, bakers and a fishmonger who makes Scrooge look like a court jester. There's the typical selection of the best and worst of the British high street – Greggs, Pret, Ole & Steen and a bubble tea place. The new energy comes from the street food though, with stalls ranging from Korean, Japanese and Vietnamese to Egyptian and Jamaican, all the way to tikka wraps and pan-American burritos. I go straight to Pho Real, my favourite Vietnamese sandwich spot in London, indexing hard as it does on its Northern Hanoi style of banh mi, which sees perfectly grilled pork that has bathed in a marinade that delivers serious flavour layered up with plenty of pickled veg and coriander.

In addition to all of the above, there is a new sort of offering here, and the street food market isn't the end of it. As you go down to the Thames, there are carts selling a very specific type of noodles. One offers hand-pulled noodles with a short rib broth, its complexity of flavour belying the broth's lightness. This is remarkable Chinese cooking, traditional in a place a long way from here, but enticing too, and far from what you'd find in an old-school Cantonese takeaway. I've been before and taken a steaming bowl down to the river, a good thing to enjoy on a cold morning. There are chewy bits of beef in the broth, and part of me always flinches in fear of biting into cartilage, much as I enjoy it when I do. This is not yet 'foreign' food that has become British, much as it is only a few degrees of separation away from the phos and ramens that are close to becoming staples. At the other noodle cart, beef and pork tripe with fiery and crispy chilli-based sauces are tossed through chewy gelatinous noodles. I'd like to see more of these places on high streets and markets outside of London.

Back in the market, my banh mi is ready and I take it to a low church wall to watch the comings and goings of the market.

I am struck by the scents. They will have changed hugely over the centuries, of course, and over the last few decades too, but today I am struck by the ancient and the new. On his corner, the fishmonger emits a low pong that won't have changed much in centuries, and to his right the sweet stench of yesterday's rotting fruit and veg emanates from the spot where the bins are collected. Above all that, though, the sweet reek of grilling meat and the heady spices of the Egyptian marinades and the curry goat next door to the fishmonger's suggest a more modern market, the one that I recognise from my interactions with it.

As with any food market, the fruit and veg sellers are some of the most reliable suppliers in the city. One stall is run by a true-blue British greengrocer, all cor blimeys and guttural shouts to attract trade, but the three remaining stalls are run by men from Turkey, the Middle East and North Africa. Where the British greengrocer stocks a typical range of British fruit and veg, these lads thrive on responding to market demands, on seasonality and on trusting their gut. This is not a high-end celebration of seasonal British veg; it is everyday and mundane, with produce priced to be bought, regularly, by all comers.

London

They want to know what you want, and why. Ask for an ingredient you found in a niche cookbook and they'll get it in for you; if others buy it too, you'll notice it again the next time you come. If not, it will disappear, though they'll get it again if you ask.

Today, as I wander among the stalls, I marvel at the fruits, chillies, herbs, gourds and berries. The breadth of herbs, chillies and aubergines suggests Middle Eastern cooking, while the plantains, yams, sweet potatoes and Scotch bonnets point to Caribbean food; the gourds suggest South Asian cooking, other herbs and chillies point to South East Asia. The thick fennel bulbs, big garlics and little courgettes remind me of Italy, the long red peppers of Spain, the green peppers of Turkey. I feel sad that there's a limited selection of greens, despite the time of year being favourable for them. One thing I notice is that there are only two types of potato – big white ones and small yellow ones. I consider that potato consumption might be one of the most affected by changing tastes in British food. I almost never buy potatoes – if I'm having carbs at lunchtime it'll mostly come from some sort of bread, and in the evening it will almost always be rice, pasta or noodles. Many older Brits would find that baffling. My father, for instance, would like a potato dish in some form at every meal he sits down to. But if the offerings at Kingston Market are anything to go by, it seems that for my generation and those younger than me, potatoes no longer play a major role in what we choose to eat.

And so with potatoes on my mind – if not in my shopping bag – I'm walking home. I pass the noodle van and cross a typical municipal park. It's not particularly warm and the threat of rain is in the air, but as I cross the park, there are groups of friends, couples, some people on their own, eating their lunch. Plenty seem to be eating sandwiches – no surprise, as data indicates that some 56 per cent of Brits eat a sandwich almost every day of the week. There are lots of people eating sushi, too. A few have falafel wraps from a spot nearby, and others pick at salads or leftovers in Tupperware containers.

And so that is us. Sandwiches at lunch aside, there's no dominant cuisine on display here – which seems to be the case in the UK as a whole. We like bread and pastries, we like food from elsewhere, and if we like your food we'll make it our own.

Before I finish, I want to make sure I'm not being myopic, leaning too heavily on one suburb and telling the story I want to tell while ignoring the bits that might suggest something else entirely. So I decide on a sojourn to my old stomping ground around Kingsland Road and Dalston, in East London.

I jump on the train and then the trusty overground; arriving at Dalston Junction I resolve to walk around until I feel I've learned as much as I can learn about how the area has changed in the decade since I moved away.

At first glance it feels like nothing has changed. I

walk down to where Stevie Parle once had a restaurant, Rotorino. It closed a while ago and has been replaced by a natural wine and small plates restaurant, but that doesn't tell me much about the state of British food. Chick'n'Sours was a few doors down, but closed more recently. It had an esoteric menu of Asian-flecked fried chicken dishes, as well as some of the best sides I've ever tasted – things such as pickled watermelon salad, an approximation of a smashed cucumber salad and a green slaw made with ginger and miso. Its closure does perhaps reflect one of the trends I've seen on this journey – the phenomenon I noticed in Lounges. Chick'n'Sours launched in 2015, at which time the use of miso and gochujang, referencing Szechuan dishes, and Thai-influenced watermelon salads were novel ideas worth going out of your way for. Fried chicken sandwiches were very much an up-and-coming trend back then. Korean fried chicken itself hadn't yet reached the mainstream, and the internet obsession with spicy fried chicken sandwiches was two or three social media influencers' endorsements away from being all-conquering. Now, a Lounges will have on its menu a close approximation of a Chick'n'Sours dish, as will plenty of other places, just nowhere near as good. It is by no means a failing of Chick'n'Sours , but the fact that this is now a commonplace dish – and priced as a daily commodity as opposed to a speciality – has spelled the end for places that were once ahead of the curve.

I carry on and note Berber & Q, a North African

and Middle Eastern barbecue restaurant that was white-hot, the centre of the food scene when I last lived here. It is still busy enough from what I can gauge, but it doesn't have the alluring aura that it once did. Does that suggest a waning of interest in Middle Eastern food? I don't think so. Does it reflect the constant hype cycle in London, driven by new, ever more recherché openings, especially out here, at the gateway to the thriving east? Almost certainly. Does it perhaps also point to a deepening of London's interest in Middle Eastern food, so that people seek out increasingly specific foods from hard-to-discover places rather than tick a Middle Eastern box? For a small portion of the restaurant-going public in East London, sure.

Having reached the towpath of the Regent's Canal, I walk west and come across Towpath, a once idyllic café that now suffers from two-hour queues. Again, not in any way its fault – its trendiness the result of the perfectly calibrated discovery feature of social media, so that droves who would once have had to work harder to discover it flock here; everything Towpath touches is delicious, so of course it has continued to increase in popularity. What I can tell you from scanning their current menu is that their brand of perfectly pitched pan-European, ingredient-led dishes is as enticing and clever as it always was. For me – and for this book – though, there's little to learn, so we move on.

Doubling back on myself, and walking back up to street level, I head north, aiming for one junction in particular. On the way I pass new restaurant after new restaurant. For a while I try to list them; some will survive, some won't, and standing here now, scribbling in my notebook, I have no idea which will be which. I cannot spot a pattern – some are trendy-looking bars, some small restaurants, most likely serving dishes on small plates. There is no discernible pattern of cuisine or style. I am sure most are good, but I am even surer they will one day be changed for something else. All of which brings me to the junction of Kingsland Road and Shacklewell Lane. Here sits Umut 2000, a typical ocakbaşı which is my favourite in the city – probably the world. Across the road is a restaurant called Mangal 2. There is also a Mangal 1, the original, once owned by the same people, and which some claim was the first ocakbaşı of its kind in London. So this junction is the place that kickstarted Britain's love of Turkish grill. The word ocakbaşı means 'fireside' in Turkish, and refers to restaurants centred around an open charcoal grill, where skewered meats are cooked over live flames and served with flatbreads, salads and pickles. At the time, this cooking and this food was unfamiliar to most Londoners, while being deeply rooted in Turkish and Kurdish communities. Ali Dirik was a pioneer in bringing this authentic Anatolian grilling culture to London, and in doing so popularising the ocakbaşı format in the UK. This area is still a centre of Turkish and Kurdish cooking in London, and there is an inexhaustible list of good spots to seek out round here for those who are inclined. What is of particular interest to me though is that Mangal 2, the restaurant that Ali Dirik decided to focus on when he sold the original Mangal in the early 1990s, is now run by his son Ferhat. Having taken over from his father, Ferhat has made the decision to move away from the staple ocakbaşı menu and bring everything that he's learned about food during a lifetime in hospitality to the menu. The result is one of the world's most visionary Turkish restaurants – a very exciting thing indeed. What that means is that out go lamb ribs, grilled quail and chicken wings cooked over the grill, and in come Cull Yaw Köfte with Grilled Apple, Oyster Mushroom Iskender Kebap, Stone Bass with Mussel Bulgur and Fermented Kapya and Ex-Dairy Beef Rib with Çemen Butter and Seasonal Greens.

Neither of these places are on my route today, but there are other restaurants that have gone through similar metamorphoses over the past few years. Singburi, once of Leyton and now in Shoreditch, could tell a similar story of a new generation reinventing a once-groundbreaking family restaurant into something that's revolutionary again. With Singburi, the evolution has allowed the first generation to retire and the second generation – as in Mangal 2 – to take what their parents established into a new era. In both instances it is a development that promises to embed some delicious and exciting dishes in the future of British food. And perhaps this is what this part of London has taught me. We've been an island defined by migration and immigration for as long as we've existed, and it's given us heritage restaurants and food cultures from all corners of the globe. Whether they originated one hundred years ago or just last week, a select few will become stalwarts, and thus new generations will be brought up in those businesses, influenced by their heritage and by the madness of London and its ever-changing food culture. Today, tomorrow and the day after that, new ideas, new dishes will be born into the British food landscape. They might look the same as they always did and we might take them into our cuisines wholesale, but more likely still they will look unrecognisable to us – and to the generation or the community that birthed them in the first place – before being absorbed into our lexicon.

So, while I cannot pin the British food in London down, I can see where the future has come from – and where it is still coming from. If Mangal 2 and Singburi are anything to go by, it will be delicious.

10

Conclusion

Next day, still exhausted from my journeys around Britain, I decide to take myself into central London for a celebratory breakfast. A chance to pull the strands together in my mind and review my conclusion. Make sure I haven't missed too much.

Under normal circumstances I would head to the original River Café – not the Michelin-starred Italian restaurant in Hammersmith, but an Italian, family-run traditional British caff, and a place I have spent the morning of my birthday for the last ten years. Today, though, I want something with more shiny silverware, perhaps even a cloth napkin. This rules out my other stalwart caff choices, the Regency Café in Pimlico, once the pinnacle but recently under new ownership, and Terry's in Bermondsey. I could head to the Wolseley, but since its founders were forced out in a corporate coup by new investors I struggle to summon the same sense of calm when the dining room there is bustling about me. I have heard that Adam Byatt's steady hand on the menu at Brown's Hotel has made it just the ticket, and the breakfast menu alone is a thing to be marvelled at. Eggs Albemarle with smoked eel, boiled eggs with Gentleman's Relish soldiers, a bacon sandwich, smoked salmon and scrambled eggs, a crab crumpet with hollandaise, porridge with prunes and a brûléed brown sugar top – all served on fine white porcelain with hotel-style silver salvers, platters and the like. It's expensive, but I've just finished a book, so treat yourself, I think; this is a solo endeavour, and I'm sure funds can stretch to a slap-up breakfast.

Seated in the drawing room, there is a pleasing whiff of floor polish that places me very specifically in a fine British tradition. Everything is on point. The menu is placed before me and my eyes land on the most contemporary British breakfast dish I could have asked for. I hadn't spotted it earlier and I won't be ordering it – in fact, a little part of me rankles at its inclusion. Despite my love of reinvention and new dishes, there is a part of me that still subscribes to a degree of respect for authenticity in places like these. But it's obviously going to be good, and it couldn't speak more to British food as it is now. It is shakshuka, a dish that has had a growth curve similar to a popular soft drink – it had a meteoric rise in popularity a decade ago before plateauing and eventually joining the ranks of other time-worn staples like falafels, labneh and flatbreads, cinnamon buns and the proliferation of bao. And here it is. Shakshuka, or Adam Byatt's version at least, has two eggs, pipérade doing the work of the traditional tomato and pepper base, a

Conclusion

mint and yoghurt dressing on top, and warm roti served alongside. Now I will not be entering into a diatribe on shakshuka, but safe to say it's a dish simple enough that you'll find a thousand variations on the traditional Maghrebi recipe. If there's minced lamb or courgette, Tunisia, Egypt, Libya, Morocco or Israel are your likely source; further afield we might find Turkish menemen, Italian uova in purgatorio, Syrian jaz maz. There are even certain versions of Andalusian huevos a la flamenca or Mexican huevos rancheros that have clear lineage to this tradition of combining eggs and tomatoes.

What *we* do, however – and it used to make me angry, but nowadays I just find it British – is take the ingredients we love, the cooking skills we've learned and our idea of a dish from somewhere else, and create a new version, often frustratingly without changing the name, so that with a squint it might be similar to the original inspiration, but more often than not it is something entirely new. It's not authentic and it would fall flat when tested against the real thing – and that used to make me upset, embarrassed for us British food writers and recipe developers, but now I realise it's just how things move around the world. Always have done, always will do. Like every other take on shakshuka, this is just our take on the dish. I just wish we'd come up with a new name, and avoid the disappointment of a customer ordering one thing and getting something else entirely. Be it at Lounges in Wilmslow or Brown's Hotel in Mayfair, though, nothing is more British.

And so as I sit here, a black coffee and the porridge in front of me, eggs Albemarle queued up to arrive next, I reflect on what I've learned. The first thing to acknowledge is frustration. My hypothesis heading out on this tour of the country was that the guy ropes tethering British food to some sense of tradition had been untied, leaving our culinary heritage flapping aimlessly in the wind. In response, globalisation and waves of migration since the war had led us to fashion new ropes made of myriad influences, and we had thus refastened our cuisine. Of course, guy ropes made of bits and pieces of this and that won't have the strength to hold down an entire nation's cuisine for ever. And so, as new influences arrive, or as we travel and taste things and bring back treats from abroad, I'd imagined a slightly random schedule of repairs had taken place – a guy rope made from early Indian influence might be replaced by one made from Sri Lankan influence. A guy rope made by the influence of Caribbean workers arriving here in the 1950s might have been replaced with one fashioned from the influence of Indonesian and Filipino workers arriving to prop up our healthcare system.

I was wrong, though – we're more resistant to change than I expected, and when we do try new things we often do them lazily, or get them plain wrong. And neither is the fare that leans towards tradition in good shape, though the exceptions that prove the rule – Cornish pasties, seafood on all our coasts and the sort

Conclusion

of quality butchery I encountered in Yorkshire – are, in fairness, outstanding. We've lost our tethers to the old ways. The oral tradition of sharing recipes is quieter, and so too is our nostalgia for them. There is a void, though, and at times it felt that the only places serving the country's trad tastes were the supermarkets and the high-street chains. And so the tail is wagging the dog, and the new wave of pop-ups and trends is dictated by finance and by algorithm.

In 1950s Britain there was a national cuisine and the supermarkets and high-street food businesses had to compete to deliver it to the British people in the most delicious, efficient or cheap way possible. On top of that we had people who had recently arrived from elsewhere and the inheritance of imperial cuisine, both of which brought new dishes to the national repertoire. Again, supermarkets and the high street followed, for the most part. Now, though, the scales have tipped so that up and down the country those who are young and reliant on their local provision of shops end up eating a pallid diet of processed foods that offer no real thrill aside from a spike – and crash – in blood sugar. The same chap forty years ago might have had a similarly simple diet, but some of it might at least have been home-cooked. Mince on Mondays, shepherd's pie and peas on Tuesday, ham, egg and chips on Wednesday, pasta bake on Thursday, fish and chips on Friday, a curry on a Saturday night and a roast on a Sunday. Do we want to return to that? Probably not, but my dismay for much of the trip has stemmed from how we've struggled to replace it with something better.

As I've driven the length and breadth of the country I have listened to a lot of radio, and particularly to the BBC national stations. We all know the roster. Radio 1: mass appeal pop. Radio 2: mass appeal pop for slightly older people. Radio 3: classical music. Radio 4: high-falutin chatting. Radio 5: sporty chatting. And 6 Music: for people who think they have better taste than everyone else. And it struck me that, for a seamless and pleasurable drive, you need to align the radio station to your mood and to your surroundings. Listening to Radio 3 while you're on the Leeds Road into Bradford finishing off the remnants of a Big Dripper burger doesn't feel right. Yet then, when winding along a ridge at altitude in the middle of Wales, it feels perfectly aligned. And I've ended up travelling the country with this strange audio synaesthesia, and it led me to realise that I might be at odds with how others feel about a thing, be it a reaction to a place or whether a posh sausage roll is really superior to a bog standard one. Funny how it's taken me forty years to realise that.

And so as a nation, if my radio station synaesthesia is anything to go by, a good chunk of us want Radio 1 style, easy, pleasing food that does a job of making us feel superficially happy for a few moments. And while that sounds judgemental, it's a valid choice. Some people want something slightly more considered, though, and these might be the folk who listen to Radio

Conclusion

2 and who make their own vinaigrette and buy cheese in a deli. Radio 3 listeners might be those who are still making wartime teatime treats, and Radio 4 might be your Islington-based foodie who supports local makers, shops from the women's collective and the health food store and is earnest about Eritrean food and the plight of grape pickers in Macedonia. Radio 5 Live would be the people lamenting the closure of pie and mash shops and the price of pints at football matches, and 6 Music would be the hipster who loves banh mi and hand-pulled noodles and seeks out third-wave coffee wherever they go. Where you sit on that spectrum will affect how you feel about British food – and where I sit on it has certainly affected how I have felt on this journey.

So I suspect I'm a dominant part 6 Music, with a good chunk of Radio 2 and Radio 4; I'm intrigued by Radio 3 but usually turn it off quite quickly when the talking gets boring, and when no one's looking I am happier listening to Radio 1 than I would ever freely admit.

These are slightly silly stereotypes, so it would be hard to say categorically how many of us go in for one thing and how many of us are after another. There's no doubt we're an odd bunch, but any nation is when taken as a whole. We're keen on deliciousness, that's clear – and happy to borrow it from wherever it exists. I came into this journey as someone who wanted British cuisine to be like a compilation CD, 'Now That's What

I Call British Food'. The very best of what we have now. I thought that when we adopted something new, it should be authentic, and that we should have finessed our old classics so that they are everything they should be, with a little extra modern pizzazz. I've realised, though, that this would make for a rather boring food culture.

Tony Blair once called Britishness having 'an equal desire to be apart from and to be a part of', suggesting a simultaneous desire for both individuality and belonging, and I've felt similarly as I've travelled around. I adore our culinary landscape, but simultaneously want no part of much of it. We often cock up what we had and make bastardised versions of what we bring in – and yet there's sometimes magic in what's created. For every cynical restaurant trying to capitalise on an anglicised version of someone else's cuisine, there's a community doing something authentic and finding an audience for it. We might enjoy a Frankenstein meal drawn from the world's larder one day and a very British meat pastry the next, and we find pleasure in both. You can travel from town to town trying variations on a thing, be it parmo, pasty or pie; there'll be inevitable differences, but we more often celebrate the quirks and differences than starting a fight about the authenticity of a classic. And when push comes to shove, serve a Brit something with a bit more spice than they might normally eat and they'll eventually get a taste for it. We're magpies; we make mistakes, but we're open to trying something that

Conclusion

looks good. I love British cuisine and what it might become – I just still don't quite know what that might be.

Acknowledgements

To my wife and son – thank you for enduring so many of these trips with me only to be unceremoniously wiped from the record in the name of narrative clarity. You were there even when the book pretends you weren't.

To my saintly editors Nick Humphrey and Jon Petre – thank you for the patience, guidance, good taste and positivity that you unfailingly displayed whenever I failed to summon any of the same myself. This book is better and considerably more coherent because of you.

To my agent Jack Fogg – thank you for taking a chance on me, for shepherding this lilting fledgling project into something resembling a real book, and for navigating much of Essex at my side.

To Annie Lee – thank you for making sense of a manuscript that arrived shaggy and unruly.

To Sarah Kennedy, Audrey Kerr, Robert Loyko-Greer and the wider team at Profile – thank you for everything I know you did for me and the book, and also for all the quiet, invisible work I'll never fully understand that was crucial in bringing this thing into the world.

And finally, thank you to Bob and Marianne Benton for indulging a hapless author in need of a comfortable armchair in the corner of a quiet room to get the last of this over the line.